Lights Out

Surviving the 70s with UFO

Martin Popoff

Lights Out

Surviving the 70s with UFO

Martin Popoff

First published in 2017
by Wymer Publishing
Bedford, England
www.wymerpublishing.co.uk
Tel: 01234 326691
Wymer Publishing is a trading name of Wymer (UK) Ltd

ISBN 978-1-908724-57-1

Printed and bound by
CMP Ltd, Dorset, England

A catalogue record for this book is available from the British Library.

Cover design by The Andys.

Contents

Preface

Alas, dear readers, I always agonise over what to say in these introductions, even though I've written now near 70 of them, I reckon. But this one, to be sure, must serve the purpose of explanation. What you're about to read, of course, is the story of the catalogue of the illustrious UFO, second wave British rock royalty in there with the likes of Judas Priest, Queen, Rainbow, and most comparatively, Thin Lizzy, but in all cases, only the catalogues of the '70s.

Now, for those of you who know—or don't know, hell, everybody, I guess—I wrote the first ever book on UFO back in 2005. *Shoot Out the Lights* looked at the entire catalogue up to that point, but since then, I've interviewed the guys many more times and have gathered much more research, to the point where merely updating that book would make it too thick, too much of a slog, more importantly too weighty for sensible publication. As some of you may know, I've done the Thin Lizzy story in three parts, the Deep Purple story in two parts... heck, actually the Deep Purple story *twice* in two parts! So, given the substantial amount of new material I had gathered for all eras of UFO, and given the fact that the band pretty tidily started in 1969 and then in 1979, called to a close the Michael Schenker era, I figured that chunk of time was an appropriate span to cover over the course of one tight, not too weighty volume.

And so that is how this book was born, with, frankly, vague plans to perhaps do a second volume that covers the Paul Chapman years up to whatever the current state of the band is at the point that I might embark upon such an undertaking. Of course, it must be said that all of this is happening because *Shoot Out the Lights* is long out-of-print and also at this juncture, something like four or five albums out of date.

So there you have it, what you're about to read is a book lovingly assembled in my usual style, where it's very much about the music, the songs, one at a time, the album covers, the production, a little bit of lyrical interpretation here and there, the studios, the creative process. For those who know my books, that's what I've always been most interested in, helping the reader appreciate those little works of art that they bring home from the record shop.

And what a catalogue this is. Now, I must preface any sort of hysterical praise with the fact that I never did cotton onto the first three records, the albums of the Mick Bolton era, too enthusiastically. However, the story of those records is necessarily here, including the strange happenstance that UFO actually was a band that was big in Japan, and Germany as well, and not so big in America or right at home in the UK, over the course of those years, sort of 1970 to 1972.

But with the arrival of Michael Schenker into the band, UFO would progress rapidly. If *Phenomenon* is a bit dour outside of smash classics "Doctor Doctor" and "Rock Bottom," no self-respecting rock fan would say the same about any of the rest of the albums through the '70s, a catalogue that culminates in *Strangers in the Night*, a double live record that many studious rock fans figure is one of the top handful of greatest live albums of all time. And yet still, UFO never garnered a single gold record in the US (hell, even Thin Lizzy eked out one), nor were ever that big in the UK. Sure, there was the continued Japanese and German success, but as history would have it, UFO would become one of these steady, prolific major label acts that everybody just assumed was bigger than they were. And hence they suffered the slings of arrows, some of which, granted, came from their rock star looks and behaviour, maybe even the posh, aristocratic, rarefied feel of those Hipgnosis cover arts.

And so this book was a rewarding project, fairly effortless to write, given all the happiness UFO songs have sent my way over the years, aided and abetted by how much fun it is to talk to the boys making the music. Kindly, funny, intelligent, the guys in UFO make interviewing stress-free. And, perhaps surprisingly, that goes for Michael as well. There have been ups and downs in talking to Michael over the years (mostly in the area of awkward silences), ups and downs that are nowhere near as extreme as his own ups and downs. But over the last decade or so, Michael has been transformed. He's engaging and introspective in interviews to be sure, but beyond that, he's become a creative juggernaut, cranking out top-shelf albums at will, regularly, rapidly, to the point where if I had to pick any kind of band one might call a heritage act, and say something to the effect that, "This is the best one of these from the last twenty years," it just might be the Michael Schenker Group, or whatever name he wants to stick on all of these gorgeous recent records.

And speaking of interviews, you might notice the curious note I've stuck in the back after the list of interviews I've done with the band. I still shake my head, but yes, somehow, I believe through email, I wound up setting up an interview with Phil Mogg, only to wind up talking to... an imposter! I thought it so odd that once I started talking to the guy, I just had to go through with the thing. It was too painful to ever transcribe, and I don't think it went more than about ten minutes anyways, but ain't that the weirdest thing? And then, to compound the matter, a couple weeks later or whatever, a couple guys who knew me said that they were on a plane, and some dude was sitting next to them impersonating me, talking about all these books he'd/I'd written and all these rock stars he'd/I'd met. Was it the same person? I simply don't know.

Anyway, I think I've said my piece here. I hope you enjoy this book. Truth be told, it might be the first of me taking some of these full-career books I've done on bands, and breaking them up to provide focus on a specific period, naturally, starting with the early years. I can't think of a better band to start with than UFO, and I hope reading this sends you scurrying back to the catalogue with a renewed appetite for deep and studious listening to all of these timeless anthems UFO have given us over the years.

Martin Popoff
martinp@inforamp.net, martinpopoff.com

Chapter One
1

"What's under the carpet?"

In what is an interesting case of life returning full circle, the UFO that we have today, always-identifying guitar slot filled by American Vinnie Moore, finds itself exploring and paying homage to the band's British blues boom roots from fully 50 years ago. However, if we didn't have Phil Mogg & Co.'s first three records—namely *1, 2: Flying* and *Live*—we might not have ever known of these fecund caveman rock beginnings, given the transformation that was to come when a certain young and very blond German axe-mad hot shot joined the band in 1973 and turned the rock world upside-down with a little something called "Rock Bottom."

And so yes, back in 1969 a band was born in Britain, not much of a band, but one that would take flight five years hence, with UFO to become one of the finest and fan-felt fondest of the British hard rock '70s, a band whose name is associated, as I say, with the likes of Judas Priest, Rainbow and most directly Thin Lizzy as second generation, latter-'70s heavy-ish metal bands laying the groundwork for the New Wave of British Heavy Metal.

Formed in northeast London by an 18-year-old Pete Way and his co-worker Mick Bolton, the band—at this point called The Boyfriends—gamely, like the punks a decade later, learned their bashing musical trade on the job. "Mick Bolton, well he's my friend, actually," reflects the storied bassist 35 years later, recalling those days. "It's a bit like, 'You play guitar? I play guitar.' That whole thing. 'Do you play guitar? Who do you like?' You never think you're going to be any good at it and I was never any good at it, like playing. It's a bit like, 'Well, I can't really play six strings; don't know how to tune it.' That sort of thing. You sit around and you put on records by The Who or The Move, Yardbirds, Kinks, Pretty Things. 'I just learned how to tune the guitar today!' And then you start. Everything was just trying to write songs. It's very difficult to look back on that without saying, 'My God!' You just have to have tremendous enthusiasm to play music. With me, that's all I ever really wanted to do. I couldn't actually see myself doing much else. I never have done, actually."

The Boyfriends, a trio featuring Pete, Mick and drummer Tick Terrazo, logged their first gig at a fashion show at Waltham Abbey Town Hall, having been mentored by Johnny Holiday of Johnny Kidd & the Pirates fame. Terrazo was soon out of the mix, replaced by Colin Turner, the band now to be called The Good, The Bad & The Ugly, a moniker that obviously served as inspiration for that of a certain album by Way's post-UFO band, Waysted, two decades later.

But in August 1969, a carpet-layer from Warminster named Phil Mogg, 21 years old at the time, became part of the mix, Mick Bolton having found him, promptly bringing him into the band house in Bounds Green, North London. "Working class, yeah," says Phil, painting a picture of his formative years, "schoolboy boxing, straight into Soho at 15, the nightclubs, that sort of life, but more as an observer than an, 'Excuse me, I am part of this fucking life—get out of my way.' More like, 'This is interesting; let's see what's under this.' You know, 'What's under the carpet?' kind of thing."

"It was really by accident," continues Phil, of his collapsing into a cursed career in the music business. "As a kid, I tried playing the drums and I was useless at that. Then I switched to bass and tried to be Jack Bruce, but I wasn't very good at that either; so I just went out working at different jobs. I moved into a house with three other guys who were in a band. Those three guys were Pete Way, Mick Bolton, and Andy Parker came later. They were going into the studio to record a pop single for Beacon Records, which was a small indie label, and they asked me if I'd like to do some singing for them. I told them I could sing, and when I went into the studio with them I totally froze! That was my debut performance."

"After that, we kind of got things together," continues Mogg. "We had a guy managing us who was in a group called The Pirates and we did little gigs and stuff. Later, we did an album in the evening because we all had day jobs. That album was UFO *1*, which was done on a four-track machine and cost us about £500. For some strange reason, they released that and the song 'C'mon Everybody' did really well in Japan, and we had another song do well in Germany. The album sounds awful. I couldn't understand it. We were sort of whisked off from playing The Marquee for six nights in a row to doing big tours in Japan and Germany."

The deal with the EMI-distributed Beacon that Phil alludes to came about through an encounter with the label's Noel Moore at the UFO club in October of '69, the story of which get retold by Beacon higher-up Derek Abrahams in the liner notes to the band's debut album, Abrahams expressing essentially that the band was young but fast learners.

Phil goes on to cite the band's early influences as "Free, Humble Pie, Led Zeppelin—these were all bands that were playing around at the time. But we were weaned on the Yardbirds, Clapton, Mayall, Ten Years After and The Animals like everybody else. But Led Zeppelin was the heaviest, because they basically took Jeff Beck's *Truth* album and doubled up on the guitars. Just the way it was done, the way Jimmy Page recorded it… it still sounds very in-your-face today."

Specifically on the topic of vocal influences, Phil cites "old artists like Screaming Jay Hawkins, Sonny Boy Williamson, Muddy Waters and Howlin' Wolf—this whole kind of section. More modern, there was Screaming Lord Sutch and Stevie Marriott was one of my favourite singers, and Arthur Brown I used to really like. Then, Joe Cocker and Terry Reid; they're from the same period."

"We were living in a place in London," continues Phil, on those early space rock days, "me, a guitarist and a bass player, when we had just formed the group. And we were going down The Roundhouse when it was all acid rock. Pink Floyd was there and Jimi Hendrix had just come over and Free had just started. So we was between doing that kind of spacey stuff but then more blues-based; we started to lean more towards R&B and blues. We'd been playing for a very short time; we didn't actually have any direction. Literally, when we got the contract to do the album, we'd never been in the studio, we'd just played The Marquee. It was the first time, our biggest gig. There was our first shot at writing and recording, and then we started writing more, and had a big transition when Michael Schenker joined the band. But before that, we were signed to a record company called

Beacon, and that was the company that put out this "space rock"—whatever it was—album, and then we got a deal with Chrysalis."

After recording with Equals guitarist Eddy Grant under the moniker of Acid, at least one song called "Take Me Higher" (unreleased), losing Colin Turner for Andy Parker, and changing their name yet again to Hocus Pocus, the band entered 1970 as UFO, named after the legendary psychedelic club that was the inspirational and influential launching pad for many a young rocker soon to rule the '70s. Grant would be instrumental in getting the band hooked up with Beacon Records.

Eventually, as Phil explained to Record Collector, the record deal came 'round. "We got a crappy deal with Milton Samuel's Beacon Records for a single with string accompaniment, 'What Greater Love?' We were so pleased; it was only after we thought 'Do we get paid?' we got £400 but, after an hour of being plied with Bacardi, we'd forgotten what we went for!"

It's time to hear now from drummer Andy Parker, and at length, given that he, like Phil, was there at the beginning and is back in UFO right now, having drummed on every record of the Vinnie Moore era of the band but one.

"Right before I joined UFO, I was in a little college band, a blues band that used to play Elmore James and stuff," recalls Parker, explaining the blues boom roots of the band. "The blues was very prevalent, with Status Quo, Peter Green, John Mayall, Clapton; it was a very bluesy period, the late '60s. Phil was always into Howling Wolf, which is interesting, because, like I say, it's come full circle. I hear a lot of that now in our recent albums. Muddy Waters and things like that. Phil is a wee bit older than me, and he had quite a good record collection in that respect, these more obscure blues artists. And so the band started there, with that blues phase that we went through. The thing about UFO, it wasn't planned. I think a lot of bands planned to do the right stuff at the right time sort of thing. UFO was never like that. We just followed our hearts and just went where it sent us. So there was a lot of blues influence early in the band. When Michael hit, the flavour of the band changed a lot. He was a rock player but a very melodic rock player. I always liked him and he was very good with melodies."

Andy, from a musical family, had started playing drums at the age of seven, although he didn't get a set to call his own until he met the guys in UFO. His entrepreneurial father, however, was not supportive of Andy's desire for a career in music, one that had been cast in stone, just like school chum Pete Way, through the discovery of Led Zeppelin. As for coming up with the name UFO for this brash new band, Andy confirms the tale that the name came from the famed UFO club, key locale of the psychedelic rock revolution.

"That's kind of where we got our name; we were searching for a name. It was not long after I'd joined up with the guys, and that club was actually closing down. It was more of an underground kind of music club, and I've never been there. I was pretty young back then so I didn't go to London to go to the clubs that much. Phillip's been there a few times. But I believe we were coming back from a gig and were driving through London and we saw all these posters out like advertising the last show at the UFO, because it was closing down. We suddenly went, 'Man that looks good in print.' It's just a very distinctive form, you know, the letters UFO. It just looked really good and we said, 'Well that's a great name; we should steal that.' So we did."

"But when I met them they were called Hocus Pocus," continues Parker, "and I think The Good, The Bad & The Ugly might have been in there too. I just remember Mick Bolton for the first time, in a pub in Hertfordshire, him going to me, 'I've got a band named Hocus Pocus' so that's why it sticks with me. So I think that's what they were called. But they had various different names. Phil was in a band called Spoon at one point as well."

Indeed as the story goes, Andy was drinking at a pub called The Golden Lion in Hoddesdon, with Steve Casey, guitarist and Parker's band mate in an act called Aurora Borealis. In walks Mick, Pete and Phil looking for a place to audition drummers, because, presumably, their current one smelled like fish. Parker found himself interested in the gig himself, when he sussed that Bolton had a Gibson Les Paul and a Marshall stack, along with a manager (Phil says he got the gig because he smelled less like fish).

"That was just a small label in London," says Andy, on the subject of the notorious Beacon Records, imprint of choice for the first three albums. "I don't know how we got with them. When I met the guys, they were involved with them already. A guy called Milton Samuel owned it. We recorded our first album with him, and then the second one, and he put the first one out the Rare Earth label in America, which was a subsidiary of Motown, I think."

This writer and everybody he knows wound up with copies of the first three albums on Nova Records out of Germany. "They were they on Nova too," says Parker. "Which was Teldec. It was a very small company so he just did deals with everybody all over the place, and then he forgot to pay us (laughs). Eventually we got the tapes handed back when they went into liquidation. But our ex-manager decided that he knew best and sold them, because he didn't see any of that money either. It's just the way things go."

If one could frame the early UFO material as not particularly impressive, it nonetheless slides into the picture as a nascent form of heavy metal. UFO *1* is not exactly *Black Sabbath*, *In Rock* or the Heep debut, but it's still subtly in that *Led Zeppelin* zone, not talent-wise, but in terms of representing a hard-hitting new take on the blues.

"There were people like Screaming Lord Sutch," cites Parker, asked about the artists who might have fired that heavy side of things for UFO, reaching back even earlier. "Those guys were heavy, and he had musicians that really kicked ass. And also Johnny Kidd & The Pirates. I mean, I don't know if you ever saw The Pirates. Johnny Spence, the bass player for The Pirates, was involved with managing us early in the day. Mick Green was the guitar player. Man, those guys were heavy as fuck! And you don't really think about it. Because it was kind of pop, Johnny Kidd & The Pirates, but those guys were heavy."

"In terms of drums, I remember Mac Poole from Liverpool. He played with Nick Simper later on in Warhorse, when Nicky Simper left Deep Purple and formed his own band. There were a lot of good musicians coming out of there. You know, heavy, man. People like Atomic Rooster kind of came up out of that, Vince Crane, from Arthur Brown, The Crazy World of Arthur Brown. That was a heavy band. There were a lot of people that you wouldn't necessarily think about."

"In fact, this is a funny thing," chuckles Andy. "I saw this ad the other day for adult undergarments, like Depends. And there was a song playing in the background. I don't know if you've seen this ad. And I go, I fucking know that song. Where do I know that song from? It was a band called Creation and it was called 'Making Time.' I thought, my God, I don't know if those guys are still alive. Because they were local where I grew up, and they used to be called The Mark Four. John Dalton, who ended up in The Kinks later, bass player, was a local guy from where I grew up and he was in The Creation. Eddie

Phillips was the guitar player, and he was the first guy I saw playing his guitar with a violin bow, long before Jimmy Page. I don't think they had the lyrics in there. I think they were just using the music, the backing track, and I thought, my God (laughs), it's being used for adult diapers. Probably the guys that wrote it need those things by now (laughs). They need the underwear. Because they would be like ten years older than me."

Further on heavy inspiration, Andy says that, "Once I joined UFO, '69, and then '70 we did the first album, we started seeing other heavy bands like Budgie around. Because, you know, you end up doing all those shows. Back then, there'd be like five bands on a show. We also used to cross paths with them now and again, bump into each other in the motorway café. But in terms of what made us heavy, let's see, Pete loved Blue Cheer; remember them? Loudest band in the world. Eddie Cochran was kind of some heavy stuff too. Phil loves Eddie Cochran and we covered a couple of his songs, didn't we? On the first album we did 'C'mon Everybody' and then 'Somethin' Else' made it on *Mechanix*. You know, I just liked the heavy drumbeats. Of course, you're listening to Ginger Baker back then. Then of course, along came my all time favourite John Bonham, and that was it, man."

After a single in May 1970, pairing "Shake It About" with "Evil," and another one three months later pairing "(Come Away) Melinda" with "Unidentified Flying Object," Beacon released the band's debut album, *UFO 1* or *1* (hereafter called *1*). In conjunction with *1*'s October '70 release date was a third single, pairing "Boogie for George" with "Treacle People," for which Phil comes up with an amusing if brief acid trip of a lyric.

The *1* album was recorded in July 1970 at Jackson Studios, Rickmansworth in Hertfordshire, which a decade later would produce Motörhead's notorious *Ace of Spades* album. A budget of £500 had been set, which was chewed up in the couple of days spent recording the album, with mix of the pretty much live-off-the-floor tracks taking place on the third day. Into April 1971, the album saw issue in the states on the colourful Tamla Motown-affiliated Rare Earth label, with Milt Samuel apparently pocketing an advance of $20,000.

The band's sound, as it emerged on *1*, cross-hatched confusingly—or maybe just unremarkably, unsuccessfully, and unwittingly—a sort of garage-style hoodlum boogie rock with a post-psych morphing called space rock, a genre which at this point might be credited to a fledgling Pink Floyd along with a small, surreal gaggle of "Krautrockers." It all sounds very high concept, but *1* is marred by simple playing, distorted, in-the-red yet muffled production, and a curious mix that is all bass guitar and drums. Phil is around, although there are long insufferable instrumental passages, but Mick Bolton is sent far away into the nether reaches of the galaxy, his guitar spare and not memorable.

Opening the record is a pastoral two minutes of introductory instrumental called "Unidentified Flying Object," which then collapses into the thundering Neanderthal hard rock of "Boogie for George."

Explains Parker, "The blues thing is kind of where met the guys and we just decided to take it a step further. I think it's where we parted company with Mick along the line, because we wanted to go a little heavier and he wasn't really that way inclined. It wasn't a personality thing; it was really just a music thing. He was still kind of like airy fairy, that trippy acid player, and we wanted to go a little bit heavier, which is why we went to Larry Wallis and then to Bernie Marsden and then finally Michael, where things really gelled, because that's just the way we wanted to go. Once again, it wasn't any kind of preordained plan. It wasn't like we need to do this so we can sell records to these people. It was just the way we were headed."

"Boogie for George," with its sort of barely written status and jammy quality, perhaps contributes to this idea that the British blues boom could bore the pants off people.

"Yeah, I mean, they would go on for a while," laughs Andy, "all those bands, Chicken Shack, Savoy Brown, Black Cat Bones. There were just so many of them. And Free came out of that. Let's not forget, I mean, that was a fucking great band that came out of that blues thing, with "The Hunter" on their first album and all that. It was like, you are blazing a trail but you didn't know it. You know what I'm saying? It's just what they wanted to do. But you look back at it now and you go, oh, you guys were heating it up. You didn't think about it at the time. It's just what we wanted to do too. It's pretty much how we've always been. The bigger amplifier you got, the heavier the sound was."

Which is a good point. A song like "Boogie for George" crossed into proto-metal as much out of amplification and distortion as anything else. Bolton's guitar, however gauzy and obscured, is dripping in electricity, and even Pete and Andy are recorded hot.

"Sure, that's right, people have said that basically the advent of PAs is a big milestone in the birthing of this heavy music, including ourselves," reflects Parker. "It started off with two columns and then four columns, and then adding to it, and then Watkins/WEM came out with this things that you could add it as you go and get bigger and bigger. And Marshall stacks... you start with one cab and you'd get a stack and then two stacks. That side of it was exponentially kind of taking off too, with people building bigger and better amplifiers. When I first started, it was these little tiny combo things with the tremolo built in, maybe a foot square, which sat on the floor. Then it was all getting bigger and better, and I remember when I first met the guys, Mick Bolton had a Les Paul and a Marshall stack and it was like, man, this is the big time."

As well, when Parker entered the game, no one was thinking about putting the drums through the PA. "No, the mic was for the singer (laughs). So to be heard you had to play loud, which is a really good way of learning to play loud. John Bonham, back then, was chucked out of places for playing too loud and he didn't have mics. You're in a little pub and you've got a great amount of welly behind it and so I was the same way. You know, get the front head off the bass drum and get as loud as you can. It's actually hard for me to play quiet. In the last few years I've been trying to hone my skills and gain a little bit more subtlety. But those early years are hard to repress."

Indeed Andy plays like a man possessed on "Boogie for George," laying the groundwork for an attack that would become necessary to keep up dynamically with Michael Schenker, once he would make his presence felt within the band. Exciting writing would require an exciting and excited rhythm section, and if anything good can be said about the debut UFO album, it's that the rhythm section is excited.

"Oh yeah, city councils had these noise level things," continues Parker, on the subject of hard-hitting. "There was this one gig we used to do in the west of England. In the back of the hall is this light bulb over the door, and as you'd play, the light bulb would get brighter and brighter. If it stayed bright for too long, boom, the power would go out. You'd kind of be watching the damn light bulb (laughs), because cutting power doesn't do you much good. Then it comes back on again and everything goes bang. So, yeah, you're watching the damn light bulb; you'd take it down and it would be like just dimly flickering, and then you'd bring it up and you'd see that thing get brighter and brighter. Oh man, you gotta take it down again."

"Because all of a sudden there's all this about, you're ruining people's hearing and the younger generation is going deaf with loud music" continues Andy. "So there's some jobsworth in the back of the hall with his sound meter and his fricking light bulb. You don't see it so much now, although I do find places where they've got a decibel level limit and if we go over, they're going to shut us down. So they are still doing it."

Back to the record, the lifeline of *1* would be the band's cover of Eddie Cochran's "C'mon Everybody," which would go on to sell over 100,000 copies in Japan, ensconcing it solidly in the band's live set for years. Amusingly, it's more or less a sister track to "Boogie for George," both essentially proto-punk '50s rock. It was considered for use because it was a less travelled Cochran song, after "Summertime Blues," which had been sent up famously by both Blue Cheer and then The Who on the well-regarded *Live at Leeds* album.

Next up is band original "Shake It About," which finds the guys toning it down for a jazzy blues with a walking bass line, before the inevitable acceleration into an electrified jam takes over. Closing side one of the original vinyl was a cover of anti-war protest song "Come Away Melinda," made famous by Tim Rose three years earlier, rendered here as "(Come Away) Melinda." True to the album's personality, the arrangement and performance is bluesy and psychedelic, bass up front in the mix, Andy ragged and laid-back, Mick texturing with wah-wah. Interestingly, Uriah Heep, on their own 1970 debut album, also covered this Hellerman/Minkoff track.

Side two begins with the rumbling and psychedelic "Timothy"—lyrically, pair this one with XTC's "Making Plans for Nigel" or to be more temporally adjacent, Pink Floyd's "Arnold Layne"—and then Pete Way's punky break-up tune "Follow You Home." As doppelganger to the latter track, the band also offer an unremarkable cover of percussive Bo Diddley classic "Who Do You Love," its nearly eight-minute girth a parched expanse of meandering basement rock.

"There will always be blues," reflects Andy, asked about yet another traditional rock 'n' roll cover on the band's debut. "I mean, there were the guys who were going to stay with that, but it was just getting harder. It was getting more edgy. If you think of Zeppelin's first album, there were so many blues songs, traditional arrangements. I wouldn't say they stole them, but you know what I mean? They were coming from the same thing as The Yardbirds and then by the second album,

'Whole Lotta Love,' they'd taken it and hardened it up, and I think that's where we were all going then. There are always trends. Like I said, mid to late '60s, the blues trend was strong and you don't necessarily follow the trend, but you can't help but be influenced by it when you're surrounded by it, everywhere you look and listen. So I think you can't help but be swayed by it somewhat."

The album's highlight however comes right at the end of the record, "Evil," courtesy of Pete Way, crossing into Black Sabbath terrain, although not so much lyrically, where the narrator laments the mischievous ways of a wandering girlfriend. Amusingly, the tale could almost be interpreted as a parent complaining about a daughter and her reckless decisions. In any event, "Evil" underscores the point that UFO was a heavy band hinting, like Free, at something even heavier, in other words, exploring ways to move beyond the blues boom into a new kind of hard rock.

Of note, this was something that Black Sabbath had already figured out with very much the same, jammy, dark, psychedelic vibe as executed by the same band configuration, namely vocals, guitar, bass and drums firing off each other with basic arrangements. That band crossed from Earth, through *Black Sabbath*, arriving at *Paranoid* and *Master of Reality*. UFO's parallel trip was from the Mick Bolton era, through *Phenomenon*, arriving at *Force It* and *No Heavy Petting*. Andy succinctly explains Zeppelin's similar path, although that band never quite put aside the blues. But as contrast, demonstrating that everyone wasn't on the same path, Thin Lizzy arrived at UFO-type music from folk, and Deep Purple arrived at UFO-type music (long before UFO), from psych. Judas Priest, despite roots back to 1969, didn't give us a record until 1974 and by that point they were already emulating hometown heroes Black Sabbath.

As alluded to, UFO's debut record featured very basic production, courtesy Guy Fletcher and Doug Flett. "They were more known as songwriters I think than producers," says Andy. "They always used to write stuff for the Eurovision Song Contest. Do you remember that, the early song contest? Yeah, always every year my mum use to go to me, 'Those chaps of yours are on again.' I'd be off somewhere, but she'd always say... We were very lucky to actually have them on our first album. It was early; I guess Beacon picked up the tab for that one—for sure, they weren't cheap that way. They were fairly well respected in the business. It was our first album and we didn't know what the hell we were doing. It's just as well we had them really, to keep us in line and tell us what was good and what wasn't."

Doug Flett, who says Guy Fletcher had nothing to do with the record, came to attention of Beacon through his association with music publisher Paul Rich, Flett being a songwriter as well as a producer. Flett not only worked out the band's contract with Milt Samuel from Beacon, but he also picked the songs that the band would cover on the first record, to augment their handful of originals.

"The one thing I can say about this band is that we never followed trends," continues Parker. "Like I said earlier, obviously trends do tend to influence you because you can't help but be caught up in them. But we were never one of those bands that said we have to make an album like this or like that, or we need to appeal to this demographic; it just wasn't our way. Basically, as you know, with this band we just play from the heart. If people like it great, if they don't then we'll try again. I think that's why I've always liked this band—they are very true to themselves rather than going, okay, this is what's in. You know it's glam rock now; we better do a glam rock album or whatever."

Chapter Two
2: Flying

"He looked like a Zulu warrior"

A sophomore UFO full-length, elaborately called, in total, *UFO2 – Flying – One Hour Space Rock* (we'll call it *2: Flying*, or more casually, *Flying*) squinted then squirted from the cellar in October 1971—the working title for the album was the more workable *Star Storm* or *Starstorm*.

If you look at the context of the times, alas, UFO were woefully behind the eight ball at this point. Uriah Heep had already released their strident debut two years earlier, not to mention *Salisbury*, which albeit is now considered a stumble en route to the magnificent *Look at Yourself* from 1971. Deep Purple had stormed the hard rock gates with June 1970's *In Rock*, and in September '71, *Fireball*, en route to *Machine Head*, issued in the spring of 1972. Black Sabbath had already trumped the sort of filmy hard blues found on *Flying* way back in 1970 with their self-titled debut and eight months after that, *Paranoid*, adding *Master of Reality* in August '71 as graphic proof of hard rock's forward strides.

Closer to the blues boom hearth, Led Zeppelin had marched their way from their pioneering self-titled debut, through to their brave and largely acoustic *III* album, set to unleash their monumental untitled fourth record a month after *Flying*'s quiet, unceremonious issue. So yes, amidst this flurry of hard rock classics, UFO proposes *Flying*, a record that did nothing to improve upon the submerged production values of the rudimentary debut, nor improve upon the band's now dated formula of turgid, meandering jams.

In the lead-up to the record, an unspecified band member told Beat International magazine, "We are now hoping to rush release our second album, because the first one now has very little to do with where we are at; we have come on so far since then. The first set was made up of two-, three-minute-long numbers which were freaky rather than heavy. I suppose that's why it caught on so strongly abroad; there was nothing quite like it around at the time. But now we are working on much longer pieces and the second album will only have three or four numbers, one of them being 29 minutes long in its pre-edited state. It's almost like a live take the way we produced it. The recordings were done at Nova Sound on their 16-track desk with Richard Dodd at the controls."

With hopeful talk like that, it seemed as if for the time being, UFO was being more so inspired by the commercially suicidal Pink Floyd of the day rather than the aforementioned nascent heavy metal acts. It is a curious assessment in a number of ways, but there's also a whiff of the aimless, even the clueless. UFO were no Pink Floyd, who themselves were no Genesis or Yes or King Crimson.

The article also reveals that the band had been thinking about adding synthesizer at this early stage, a VCS3, not surprising given the direction of the second record and the excitement around the equipment at the time with bands like the aforementioned Floyd. Expressed was also a desire to improve the band's light show, again a sensible idea for a band exploring Hawkwind-like "space rock."

Added label boss Milton Samuel, in the same profile piece, speaking about the band's success abroad but not at home, "It's simple. We reckon that if a record is any good at all, you can find a market for it somewhere and turn it into a local hit. Most companies wait until the record makes the British charts before they even try to get it released abroad, but we get all our records released in as many territories as possible. We've had singles which haven't sold 300 copies here, but which have made the chart somewhere or other in the world, No.1s in Israel, Singapore, Hong Kong, and so on." Claimed in the feature are sales of 250,000 albums and 750,000 singles, outlandish and very likely exaggerated numbers direct from Milton, especially given that at this point, we were dealing with the debut album alone.

As promised, and as if to drive a stake through their career, UFO included on *Flying* two lengthy exercises in Chinese water torture, namely "Star Storm" (18:50) and "Flying" (26:30), "probably because we were doing acid or something," laughs Pete, clarifying with, "probably because we were getting a little bit out of it on dope and stuff (laughs). I don't think we were doing acid though, seriously. But I think we were a bit influenced by that, the acid rock syndrome."

"You know," chuckles Parker, "I don't know where that came from, that whole *One Hour Space Rock*. I often wonder, how did we come up with that? What made us decide to do that? I guess it's just where we were at. Because that would've been what, '71, and I guess we were just experimenting. There was the attitude that the first album had a lot of short poppy tunes on there. The record company was cool and let us do what we wanted. There was a lot more jamming back then and there was a lot more acid going round too. People were tripping and taking mescaline and going, 'Wow, that's cool' and do a solo for fifty minutes."

Speaking with Metal-Rules, Andy said that it was "very hard for us to know how we were doing because the record company didn't tell us how much they sold. But we never got any money for those at all. All I know it that based on the amount of people that I've seen that had those albums, they sold pretty well. Not only in Germany but also in Japan too. We did the first album, UFO *1*, then we did *Flying: One Hour Space Rock* and people have asked me why and I don't know why. Because we could? The thing about this band is that it always comes from the heart. It's genuine, it's not manufactured. The *Space Rock* album was just where we were at the time. The record company told us to go do it and we just did and it was different."

"So yeah, I think those albums sold a lot, I think. The first album came out in 1970 and I remember this because when we recorded it was 1969 and I was 17 years old. Beacon Records gave me the recording contract to sign but I wasn't old enough, so my parents had to sign it for me. My parents refused to sign it because they thought I was going to get ripped-off. So I had to wait until my 18th birthday to sign the contract myself. So it came out in 1970 and I did get ripped-off. But if I hadn't done that album no one would have ever heard of me. This is the whole thing: sometimes you've got to get ripped-off to get your foot in the door."

"Flying" was distinguished at the time as the longest rock track ever recorded, 26:30 indeed testing the limit of fidelity one could get out of a side of vinyl at the time or for that matter, through the technology's domination through the ensuing twenty more years.

What's even more impressive is that it wasn't the only song on the side, Beacon adding "The Coming of Prince Kajuku" at 3:43, which, along with side one, delivered the promised one hour of "space rock." The album would be recorded at Nova Studios in London, Flett making use of a relatively advance 16-track mixing desk.

On the lyrical front, "Star Storm" finds Phil mixing galactic imagery with words of love, a muddle but an ambitious one, while "Flying" is a lengthy, dark, violent, but mostly indeterminate sci-fi saga culminating in a backwards quote from Rudyard Kipling's "Gunga Din" as well as some forward slow motion spoken effects. Incidentally, album opener "Silver Bird" also supports this sci-fi theme, with the narrator coming across a landed UFO housing a strange being who offers to take our narrator away, a proposal that he accepts.

The highlight of the album however was concise riff rocker "Prince Kajuku." "He was our truck driver," says Pete, of the goodly prince. "Yeah, he drove the van. We had the aircraft seats behind, with the equipment and he had very curly hair. He looked like a Zulu warrior, in Phil's imagination. That's who Prince Kajuku is, in those movies. Those albums... it was just us trying to write songs, really. Now, if ever I was going to own up to wondering if I could try and write hits, it was then. After those days—I was 17 then, 17-and-a-half, and I'm a bit older than that now—I wrote songs in those days where you wanted the record company to like them. Actually it goes back to everybody—you want the record company to pick you up. It doesn't matter if it's the record company owned by the bloke who runs the banana shop; it doesn't matter what record company it is. But in those days you tried to write a hit. You didn't have the luxury of going out and trying to play the blues, in fact, not that we could. We didn't really have the blues in us. It was just trying your best to write something catchy. But one thing I did is that I wanted to be like Blue Cheer or something like that."

Pete's words are exasperatingly contradictory to the way both Andy and Phil have framed the band, as well as to the recorded evidence. But he does proffer a nugget of truth in his comparison of UFO to Blue Cheer. Both Blue Cheer, on their first two records, and UFO, similarly across the handful of more up-tempo tracks on the first two records, were achieving a next level of heaviness through shaking the blues tree and then by way of distortion levels achieved through extreme if partially erroneous, production techniques.

Another amusing memory for Pete concerning "Prince Kajuku" is being on African TV, Way relating that, "The announcer comes on and says, 'Here's a band called UFO with a song called "Prince Kajuku" that will be a big hit in Nairobi!'"

Phil has confirmed Pete's recollections, adding that this particular band employee was very tall and had red hair and was nicknamed The Prince, with the nonsense word Kajuku being added later. The resulting entertaining and silly "Prince Kajuku" lyric however is unrelated to touring, Phil warning about the voodoo magic easily executed at a different sort of prince's behest. The song was issued as a single, backed, sensibly, with "The Coming of Prince Kajuku," reaching No.26 in the German charts, slightly bettering the No.30 placement of the first album's "Boogie for George."

The original UK Beacon issue of the second UFO album was considerably entertaining, graphically speaking. The front and back covers featured simple interstellar illustrations, a little funky and hippie-ish, while inside one got full lyrics as well as a dramatic picture of the band. Slight variants ensued around the world, including confusion as to the exact title of the album.

When asked how quickly those first two UFO records were put together, Pete goes with, "Blimey, maybe seven days? People had to actually go to work. It was like laying carpets and then coming back for the evening. It was seven days and vocals in an hour-and-a-half or something (laughs). 'That's all right. I can probably sing a bit better, but keep it.' The thing is attitude. Oh yeah, people had to work. Mick had to carry things in a factory, because it paid better. Because we had to buy amplifiers, don't forget. When you're 18 and you have to buy amplifiers, forget about careers. When you're 50, you'll get a pension. 'No, mate, I'll need a Marshall amplifier today, so I'll go do some work.'"

Preceding the album's release, the band mounted a promotional tour of Japan which included a handful of gigs, successful enough for the band to go back the following month, supporting Three Dog Night. Wrote Mike Guy from Melody Maker, on the verge of the campaign, "One of the heaviest groups on today's contemporary music scene is UFO, an explosive quartet which believes that hard rock has to be put over with plenty of action on stage. Not for them, the just-stand-there-and-play approach. They respond physically to the sheer power, an all-embracing feel of their material, which in turn triggers off an atmosphere of total audience involvement."

Commented Pete in the same piece, "We have noticed that people seem more into the music if you move about. When they go out to see a group, they expect more than what they can hear on a record. Movement enables us to become completely engulfed in what we are playing and we regard it as a vital part of the communication process. I suppose you could say some of it is showmanship, but mainly it's spontaneous, because we are having a ball."

The September campaign would entail a touch-down at Sapporo Airport on the 18th, a press conference at Mugen three days later, followed by a show on the 23rd at Osaka Prefectural Gymnasium to a crowd of 10,000 and another on the 25th at the Mugen Sound Festival, Hibiya Outdoor Music Hall (estimated attendance: 23,000), to be documented for a forthcoming live album, which would be sold at the same festival one year later.

"Too many rock bands think it's enough to amble on stage in tatty jeans and sweatshirts and do a moody," said Phil, in conversation with the NME, January 1972. "We try to do more than just play music—we entertain. That's why coloured soul artists always come back to popularity—they are real professionals; they put on a show."

Commented Mick Bolton on the trip abroad, "Japanese audiences are great. They will accept anything that's done well. They haven't been told what is trendy to like and dislike," to which Andy added, "We played opposite a local band called Far Out and an American soul show called Sounds 70. They had a black singer named Toile who really showed what it's all about. He was incredible—what a stage show! But if he appeared in Britain, the underground audiences just wouldn't give them a chance. You can mix bills over there but not here, which is part of the reason why there's so little work."

Expressing the band's sense of ambition, Pete said, "I think the Americans are more into being entertained. They like outrageous stage shows and we tend to go a bit berserk sometimes. What we really want to do is take the light show a stage further, because that scene was never really exploited and create a true multimedia experience. I think you need American money to do that, but obviously the ultimate aim is British success. After all, overseas hits don't mean a lot if you can't get recognition among your own people."

"We were amazed," says Andy, of the improbable trip to Japan. "We drove our van to the airport at Heathrow, our old van with all the gear in back. But when we got off the plane we got all those limousines waiting for us there; it was just so bizarre. We were stars on the other side of the world."

But the attention was warranted—the band's debut record had moved an astounding 135,000 copies in Japan, doing brisk business in Germany as well, with the UK registering only an estimated 3,700 in sales. However, continued lack of pay from the label back in the UK would soon result in the band leaving Beacon. One last record of this era would result, a live album issued in Japan as *U.F.O. Landed Japan* and in Germany as *Live*. The album would not see UK release, which was just as well—UFO would now find themselves free to look for a better deal.

Chapter Three
Live

"Out came the bottle of Bacardi"

Rounding out the catalogue of the original band, *Live* (to use the simpler and less awkward German title), featured one side covers, one side UFO originals, all recorded at the Hibiya Outdoor Music Hall in Hibiya Park in Tokyo on the band's inaugural visit to Japan. Japanese audiences, confronted with a heavily bearded Phil Mogg and the guys dressed quite flash and fashionable for the times, copped to the band's resemblance to Free, as expressed through their blues and original rock 'n' roll covers, most prevalent being "C'mon Everybody," rather than the this thing they seemed in the process of floating, space rock, and the meandering that would entail, especially given the lack of ideas, musicianship and craftsmanship within the band's ill-advised long songs.

As well, unfortunately, the live album's compositions somehow managed to drown amidst the same wincing bass-heavy production values as the two studio albums, despite being recorded a world away in Japan at the considerable cost to Toshiba Records of £10,000. At least it was all rock, essentially somewhat like a bad version of Free in relentless electric mode.

Says Phil, now summarizing the best-forgotten pre-Schenker days, reflecting specifically on those first two albums, as well as *Live*, "Oh then? I wasn't quite sure what we were doing. Knocking around, all living in a house together and going to The Roundhouse and watching bands that were coming up. Oh, it was the end of the blues boom, and it was the move from blues and R&B into psychedelia, so we was kind of caught in the middle, and I wasn't sure what we were, a blues band or we were psychedelic. We weren't quite sure, but I think we tended to lean more towards the bluesier side. The band... you would go to watch the Yardbirds, the Animals, the Jeff Beck band. Free just came out, the early Yardbirds. So we were a bit confused then. And of course, by the time Michael joined, it kind of solidified where we was actually going, or helped to shape us."

"Germany and Japan were for some reason our best markets," adds Andy. "People have asked me over the years why were those album successful in Germany and Japan and not so much in England and America? The only answer I can come up with is it must have come down to the record companies. I guess they did a better job promoting them. That's the only reason why I can think, why are we suddenly only having a hit in Japan? I mean someone must have been playing it; we didn't go there, not until we were established anyways. People knew about the record and the same with Germany. It was on Telefunkendecca, Teldec in Germany and I don't remember who it was on in Japan. On Rare Earth in America and Beacon in England. The only thing I can think of is the promo guys were doing a better job in Germany and Japan."

"But Beacon were absolute rubbish," continues Andy. "I mean we never got paid anything, even though Milton Samuel—that was the guy who owned Beacon—he was a bit of a laugh. From West Africa or maybe Jamaica; I know he moved to Jamaica quite soon after. Like I say, we did those albums for him but he never gave us any money. But every time we'd go up there to go and talk about money, out came the bottle of Bacardi and he'd go, 'Oh come on, boys, let's sit down and have a drink.' We'd talk about it and half a bottle of Bacardi later we were out on the street again, heading home and still no money. Damn, he did it again! Yeah he was a pretty smooth operator, I don't think he's with us anymore; I think he passed away several years ago. But he was a pretty interesting guy. I mean, I think his big thing is that he had that Show Stoppers song, "Ain't Nothing but a House Party"—that was a big record for Beacon."

Phil said much the same thing speaking to Circus in 1978 (in a quip that is also similar to the one he told Tim Jones of Record Collector): "We found out the truth about these people, because every time we went to the record company to say we needed a new stack of Marshalls, we'd get laced up with Bacardi rum by the company president, later realizing we hadn't talked about anything. Great strategy on his behalf."

Continues Andy, "The masters for the first albums, the Beacon albums, Beacon went into receivership and we ended up getting those masters back at some point. This is when we were managed by Wilf Wright. So they actually came back into our possession, which is after they'd been out on different samplers. Because what used to happen, every time we put a Chrysalis album out, Beacon would chop and change and put another album out at the same time, to dupe people that it was in fact the new UFO album, even though it was rehashed Beacon product. So we were kind of glad to get those masters back. Well, unbeknownst to us, our manager, Mr. Wright, sold them to a rather unscrupulous chap and sold them for money or drugs or something without us knowing. Just sold them outright, so we lost them again."

"Now several years later when I was back with the band, around the *Walk on Water* time, '95, the manager that we had then, Robin Greatex, made inquiries to see if we can actually get those back. And basically he was told that if he wanted to keep walking, to drop it. If he wants his kneecaps he would leave things alone. Yeah, so it's always been out there, you know. But we felt like we'd been out for that long, they probably used them up so it wasn't really going to hurt us anymore. Leave Wilf alone, you know."

"But we'd actually got them back, because Beacon went into liquidation. We'd been handed the tapes back, which is great, because we never got paid for them from Beacon either. So we finally got a hold of them, but I guess Wilf decided that he would do a deal, and we'd never been able to get the rights back to them ever since. And this is the closest we've ever got. So yeah, that's about as far as you want to go with those people, you know. But I think that's all kind of moving out now, isn't it? It's a whole different ballgame now. Those days of leg-breakers and arm-twisters have kind of moved on now."

Articles throughout the years seemed to be swapping the same dodgy numbers around, but for better or worse, the assertion is the following, with respect to the scope that UFO were stiffed: apparently each of the first and second album generated more than £2M in sales (not two million copies, as is sometimes cited), with the band receiving royalties of £400 for the first and for the second, to the tune of £800 total.

As for the less-distributed and less-licensed third record of the trio, *Live* opens with a raucous version of "C'mon Everybody," erstwhile glammed up by handclaps as percussion accompaniment. Bass dominates almost Lemmy-style but more bulbous, while Mick's added heavy metal power chord represents the juicing of the song for the early '70s, a marking of one's territory. As Phil calls upon "Stewart" for a new mic stand and a glass of water, the concept continues, with the band's electrocution of "Who Do You Love," although too long at 9:00. Side one of the original vinyl closes with a song not on either of the band's first two albums, a cover of Paul Butterfield's "Loving Cup." Again, the theme is adhered to perfectly. Phil calls the song "a blues number," but the presentation is more akin to Black Sabbath on the debut, or Cactus or Mountain or Free at the loud end of their oeuvre. All told, the band didn't write a single track on side one, but their interpretations spoke volumes.

Of note, an edited version of the live "Loving Cup" was used as the B-side to "Galactic Love," a non-LP UFO original issued in studio version as a picture sleeve single during this era. As for that particular rarity, it's a song in the mid-heavy zone, Mick mostly strumming jazzily on a poppy hard rocker, while Phil heavies it up through a forceful vocal and Andy, as usual, bashes up a spirited beat.

Over to side two, and *Live* is all originals, beginning with the pair of "Kajuku" songs from *Flying*, the band writing pure although distressingly simple hard rock away from boogie, essentially presaging compositions associated more with Pete Way through the rest of the '70s. A turned-up "Boogie for George" is next, followed by Pete's "Follow You Home," on which the similarities to "You Really Got Me" are admitted through a drift into that very song.

All told, very much like the studio albums—and quite amusingly—it's drummer Andy Parker who gets to go nuts most often, almost all the time in fact. And then Mick Bolton as well, he solos a lot on this record, again, sounding very much like Tony Iommi in the early days.

As alluded to, UFO was paying attention to what was going on around them, resulting in the transition to more of a modern hard rock band. Asked if the guys were being influenced directly by bands they were touring with, Andy says, "Back then we didn't really tour with bands. I mean, we just did gigs. It wasn't like we got on a tour opening for anybody. I can't remember us actually doing that until we came to America. It was pretty much just, you got an agent, you booked gigs, you went. Obviously sometimes you'd be opening for somebody at the gig, and sometimes there were people opening for you, but it wasn't like you went on a whole tour and went up and down the country with the same act. I don't remember us ever doing that."

In terms of American bands Parker was digging, "There was Grand Funk Railroad and Mountain. I remember those first couple of Mountain albums—I use to play the crap out of them; that was a great band. Back at that the time, Leslie West was Michael's favourite guitar player. I remember him going, 'For me he has the best tone.' So I mean, there was some good stuff coming out of the States. Blue Cheer, Grand Funk, Mountain… to British people that was America, you know, in a nutshell. Big and bodacious. I never saw Mountain live I have to say, but I really liked the material and I liked the guitars; it was a similar line-up to UFO. I mean, the drummer had double kicks and they had this great guitar player. That kind of music just really appealed to me. And we used to always have this roadie called Rob Willis who loved MC5 and *Kick Out the Jams*. He was always going on about MC5, but I'd never gotten to see them either."

Chapter Four
Phenomenon

"That bloke's really good, isn't he? The blond fellow"

Swift kick forward for the band, as UFO sign to Chrysalis, receive manna from hard rock heaven in a quizzical young German called Michael Schenker (b. Jan. 10, 1955), make a record called *Phenomenon* and slap on the front of it an early yet memorable piece of graphic intrigue by hip art shoppe Hipgnosis. But of course, the main piece of the new circumstance is the arrival of Michael Schenker, not, however, replacing axeman from the first three records Mick Bolton, but an interim guitarist named Bernie Marsden (from Skinny Cat), who himself pitched in after a stint by Shagrat/Blodwyn Pig axeman Larry Wallis, later of Pink Fairies and Motörhead fame, the stint with Lemmy being quite brief. Wallis would be in UFO for approximately eight months, from February '72 to October '72, with Bernie lasting from that point until June '73.

"Larry Wallis was a really interesting character," recalls Andy. "I look back fondly at the time spent with him. He was different. He didn't turn out to be the best guitarist for UFO; obviously we parted company but he was a very interesting character. He's a very good musician and from a whole different scene, that kind of scene in London with which I hadn't had much experience. You know, Mick Farren of The Deviants and Twink, Pretty Things, those guys, that was his big scene."

Speaking with Rich Davenport about the brief Larry Wallis, Pete said that, "Because we'd had the previous albums we had a popularity overseas. So they'd turn up for that. But I wouldn't say we were the

Heavy Metal Mud. Larry is a hippie psychedelic icon. He auditioned (ed. with Jimi Hendrix's "Driving South!"), and he played really good; it's just the style was different from where we were. If Larry was experimenting with us, we were happy to go along with it. We spent hours in rehearsals talking. We kind of let him tell us what we should be playing, and in the end we thought, this isn't what we want to be playing. Phil said, 'It's not working, is it?' We weren't happy with the way it was proceeding. Larry wasn't focused on what we saw. He can write a song, but it didn't fit with what we did. On and off I speak to Larry. There's never been any animosity; we moved on to a different direction."

After running through Bernie Marsden as an option, Pete related that, "Rudolf Schenker actually put it together because he spoke English; 'My brother—he will play!' I thought, the blond guy is a really good lead guitar player. And he was! He was the big chemistry that put the whole thing together, plus the fact that we got on well even though we weren't necessarily speaking the same language at the same time. We had a lot of fun in the early days."

"I don't remember whether we had any offers from anyone else," continues Andy, on the band's label deal. "I mean, that was just a godsend to get that deal because we hadn't recorded in so long, because of the problems with Beacon. We just decided we weren't getting paid and it was still new. We actually didn't record for absolutely ages, and then the way the Chrysalis deal came about, we actually had them as an agency first, because they use to have an agency as well as a record company—that's how they started. They were actually booking gigs for us 'cause we were doing pretty well. That's all we were doing; we weren't recording so we were working on that stuff going up and down the country doing gigs. Chrysalis, obviously representing us as booking agents, I guess they saw something. When they started up their label, they saw something worthwhile in us and offered us the deal. So I wouldn't like to say whether there was other people vying for us."

As for the lasting effect from being signed with Beacon, Andy told Marko Syrjala, "We got no money from Beacon Records at all, so we told them they'd broken the contract and then there was a period from like 1972 to 1974 when we didn't do anything. Then Chrysalis signed us in 1974. As I say, what happened every time we made a Chrysalis album, Beacon would remix and re-release those records with another name on them. So when people would ask for the new UFO album in the shops, they'd not get what they were looking for. It was just bad, but eventually that faded out. I think we got ripped-off really badly, but it did lead to as you see me now, forty years later."

"That was my first pro gig and I was about 20, 21," recalls Bernie Marsden, who went on to Wild Turkey (with Jethro Tull bassist Glen Cornick) and then of course bigger and better things as co-guitarist for Whitesnake, through to 1981's *Come An' Get It*. "I had had gigs offered to me before that; I had auditioned for stuff, and then I would get the gig and then realise, I don't really want to do this. One of the bands was a band called Renaissance, who did pretty well in America, and I think Canada. But if you can imagine their music and me, it just didn't fit. You see, in those days, when you auditioned for people, they kind of didn't tell you who the band was until you got in the audition. So you found yourself applying for a job you didn't want anyway. It was this thing of turning professional, you know? So that was a funny thing. You would get the gig and then you would say actually, I don't want it, and then you'd see the guys who auditioned two weeks later and they would say, 'Well, I thought you joined Renaissance?' And I'm like 'Yeah, well I turned it down.' You then get a bit of reputation where they say, you know, this guy is messing us around. There's this young kid coming in, he's a great guitar player, but he doesn't really want the gig. It was just a matter of waiting for the one I wanted to do, which turned out to be UFO."

"I was involved on the *Phenomenon* album," continues Bernie. "I was involved in some of the writing on the album. The irony of me taking that gig as my first proper gig was that it backfired on me. It got back to all the guys I messed about, because when I did join the band, we were socially incompatible, should I say in a polite kind of way—we didn't get on at all. Consequently, when I did leave, when I did quit, in fact I was the guy who kind of found Michael Schenker. I've seen many interviews where Michael's said, 'It's all bloody Bernie Marsden's fault! Because he got me into this.' But he was a great, great guitar player and I knew he was a bona fide replacement for me. So I kind of said to him, 'You should join this band, because I'm getting out. I can't stand it anymore.'"

"I was part of UFO for about ten months, a little under a year," adds Marsden. "I mean, we had kind of a pact, which I said, after I was finished, 'Look, we don't get on, we don't like each other, and I'll never say I was with you if you never say you were with me.' It kind of worked. It was almost a secret for about twenty years and then when we got older and definitely wiser, it seemed like a stupid thing to maintain. But by then, people were always saying, 'You were part of UFO!' Because there are thousands of people throughout Europe who saw me play with them. People would say, 'Did you play with UFO?' I would say 'No, no, it wasn't me.' 'I saw you! I saw you!'"

"This kind of myth perpetuated for a long time, but now with the Internet and stuff, everybody knows everything. But I was involved with *Phenomenon*. I wrote a song called 'Oh My' on the album, and I was involved with the beginning workings of 'Doctor Doctor,' so I kind of should have stuck around. I'm not on the album, but I did some demos for it, with a guy called Dave Edmunds (at Rockfield Studios in Monmouthshire—the album proper would be recorded at Morgan Studios in London). They are obviously around somewhere. They would be interesting to hear after thirty years or whatever (laughs). But it's one of those things; when you're 21 years old, there's always hundreds of other bands to join."

Pete recalls losing original UFO guitarist Mick Bolton this way. "You know what, I think a certain amount of it is, somebody's got a girlfriend and they're going to get married, a fiancé or that. Then maybe I should get a job. I don't want to be travelling in a band, go up and down the motorway. I don't know what we were earning; five pounds a night or something. It's very difficult to say, those early days. You wonder about how many people who could have been very, very successful, rich people today who decided they couldn't do it because they were spending too much time away from their fiancé."

"Bernie was in the band for awhile," says Pete, the plot thickening. "It's one of those things, really. Scorpions was supporting us and Michael was the guitar player for Scorpions. Bernie lost his passport and we had to play. And it was actually Phil who said, 'That bloke's really good, isn't he? The blond fellow' and he filled in from then on... he didn't speak English and we didn't speak German particularly and that was it. He was in the band." It must be stressed that Bernie did in fact show up for the next night's gig and that he indeed did finish the tour before Michael was formally brought into the picture in July '73, after Schenker had been encouraged to do so by the Scorpions, who were actually considering throwing in the towel.

This was all going down July 18th, 1973, with the band having to leave Bernie in London, three hours before a show in Regensburg, Germany. Before you know it, Michael is in the band and moving back to board with Phil, which lasts a couple of months. Soon the new line-up is seen on German TV (in their finest platform boots) for the first time, on Music Today, October 13th, followed by a return visit to tour Germany, yet again supported by Scorpions.

"So there we were, no guitarist and no gear," said Phil, speaking with Scene magazine. "But the show had to go on. We'd sold a lot of advanced tickets. If we hadn't gone on, they quite likely would've smashed the place up." "We wound up doing 'Gloria,' 'I'm a Man'— all the basic stuff everyone knows," added Pete. "Michael didn't speak English; even the letters for his guitar strings were different. He kept calling one H, and it's B to us."

"That was more circumstances than anything," adds Phil, interviewed by Dmitry Epstein. "Bernie Marsden, who was playing with us at the time when we had a tour in Germany to do, forgot his passport, and things weren't great. We'd seen Michael play with Scorpions—an outstanding guitarist!—so we asked if we could borrow him for the gig, and we did two nights with him and then asked him to join. But Bernie was great, Bernie was very funny—except when he took his shoes off and put them under the heater in winter. Heat used to make the car really smelly. Once he took off his shoes and fell asleep and Pete Way tied them up with plastic bags and threw them out the window so we didn't have to suffer. Bernie was good; we really had fun touring. It was that kind of tour when there's six of you in a car and you're not earning any money, so it's more fun."

Interviewed by Marko Syrjala, Pete said that, "Bernie's just an easy-going, nice guy to get on with. I think we were a little too wild for Bernie. Bernie's like 'Hello?' and we're like 'Where's the drugs? Give us a drink!' David Coverdale once said to Bernie. 'What are they like then, those guys?' and Bernie said, 'Oh, you wouldn't believe!'"

Confirming Phil's telling, Way explains, "The Scorpions were supporting us actually and we played together a lot, so we asked Rudolf Schenker if his lead guitar player would play with us. So we did a reduced set. It was because on the night there were people there and the promoter said, 'If you don't play, people are gonna go mad!' So we had to work it out and that was in the day when the songs were a lot simpler."

As for Michael's disposition, Pete says, "Michael was wild, but he became a lot moodier later, I don't know why; it's just something that happens, I think. He was good fun. I don't know what changed, but I think he stressed out and then it's the usual thing, drugs. He did change the style of the band. Bernie was very kind of blues-oriented; that's why we never did an album with him actually. What happened was Michael had a much more open style, much more sophisticated while still simple, and it gave the songs more style. Of course *Phenomenon* was the first album we'd made since Mick Bolton left. It just made the whole thing fresh. Plus he was very young. I mean I was 21 and he was 17 or 18. It was like a new beginning, so it was quite interesting."

"That was a natural progression," muses Andy, charting the course through the players up to Michael. "When we first formed and did our first album it was kind of a mishmash of stuff, but it had a bluesy kind of background to it, because that's where we were coming from, the '60s blues boom with John Mayall & The Bluesbreakers and all those bands, Chicken Shack, Savoy Brown; that's where I was coming from when I met them. And then we went into our experimental space rock thing, and then naturally we start to progress, especially when we got Michael back in '73. It was just a natural progression because he was in that genre of guitar playing. He was a harder rock guitar player than maybe we had before, because Bernie Marsden who was in the band, he was very much blues at the time. He went on to join Wild Turkey with Glen Cornick and that obviously led to Whitesnake. When Michael came along it was like, yeah man, this is what we want, coming from Scorps—they were a bit heavier weren't they? There was that heavier, Teutonic influence."

"I was touring already with the Scorpions before I joined UFO," says Michael upon his fateful decision. "That's how I met UFO, Scorpions being an opener, a special guest, for UFO. They had arrived without a guitarist and without equipment, so they borrowed me and the Scorpions' equipment and that's how they found me. I ended up playing with both Scorpions and UFO for a couple of concerts until the other guy came back; this was like 1973. And then they approached me. I always told the Scorpions that, you know, one of these days, if somebody from England approached me, I would leave and go there, because that's where all the rock music is coming from. In Germany it was very hard to develop. There was no management allowed and it was really, really... it was disco music and it was just kind of dead in Germany. So when UFO wanted me, I said, like, this is it."

"And then I just kind of made sure I wouldn't disappoint my brother too much. I found Uli Roth, and so I felt comfortable and ready to go. That was the only way I could leave the Scorpions. I had to find somebody good enough who could be there for my brother. Uli was the one I saw when I was 14 years old. He was really good and he left a really good impression on me. So when I decided to leave, I approached Uli, 'Can you please join the Scorpions?' (laughs), and he said yes, so he did it, and so I felt good about it. I mean, it was easier for me to leave that way because it felt right."

Pre-Scorpions, Michael had played with formative bands called The Enervates, Cry and Copernicus. But the level of professionalism was minimal, given that when he debuted with the Scorpions, New Year's Eve 1969, he was but 14 years old, having locked onto guitaring as a profession the day brother Rudolf came home one day with a Gibson Flying V, which was to become Michael's trademark axe with UFO and beyond.

Already Michael had in place some eccentricities to his personality that would cause an immediate and pronounced separation from the tight, laddish lads in the UFO band. First and foremost was the language barrier, but Michael's obsessed attachment to the guitar, as well as his uncommon philosophy of not listening to other people's music, something that grew more pronounced as the years went on, caused insularity as well.

Speaking with Jeb Wright, Michael explained that, "I never developed any social skills for about ten years, in the most important time too. Because I was always in my own little four walls practicing. I didn't speak any English. When I came to London, I knew this was it. I have always been a universal person. I was walking down streets in parts of town where there were white, black, green and yellow people and I felt like I was at home. The only thing I didn't like was that I could not communicate. The band was also very sarcastic. They would make sick jokes—that didn't go down to well with me. My girlfriend spoke some English, so she would explain what they were saying, if it was worth it. The drummer would tell her, 'Tell Michael that he is very lucky that he doesn't know what we are saying.' I really was lucky that I didn't know (laughs). You know, that may be why it lasted longer that it should have!"

So Michael crawled inside his guitar. "I started playing guitar when I was nine years old, but it was when I was 14 years old that I was imagining playing guitar onstage in my head, and it was based on hearing Jeff Beck and Jimmy Page. They're exceptional performers that made me decide that I wanted to do what they were doing. That was the excitement that made me want to practice and practice. I said that I wanted to be one of the best guitarists in the world, but that didn't mean anything other than I wanted to be as good as those people I felt were best. I wanted to be able to create such an effect as they had on me."

"I don't really focus on listening to music at all," continues Schenker. "If I do, I write, I invent. I especially don't listen to rock music, because I want to keep it all fresh and exciting for myself. If I listen to rock music all day long, when it's time to make an album, I'm all worn-out. It's like eating too much chocolate—you want to make sure you keep it special. But I mean, I knew exactly what I wanted. I stopped listening to other people's music when I was about 17. At that point, Leslie West was one of the last people I listened to, and that was it. I knew exactly what kind of sound I wanted. I knew that I had ideas within me to express musically. I was very shy and very much into my music and not speaking any English. It was all kind of pretty confusing and new to me. But it was the music that connected us and you know, anything to do with UFO, was for me music period."

Then there was spirituality, a background drama in Michael's life that would get wilder and more surreal in proportion to similar swings in the band's career trajectory. "Oh I started very early, I think when I was five," claims Michael. "Yeah, and in Germany also, as part of school, to be confirmed, you had to study for two years the Bible, so I got confirmed when I was 14. And when I was 15 or 16, my brother and I discovered eastern religion; it just went from there, and I just kept going in all directions."

"I simply wanted to do my own thing," says Michael, further elaborating on the break with what was to become the biggest band ever out of Germany. "I think God wanted it that way. I don't think it would have worked as well for Scorpions or my brother if I had been in the band. I think by moving me out of the Scorpions... my brother is more like a group person and I am more of an individual person. His dream was always to be in one of the biggest bands in the world and my dream was to be one of the best guitarists in the world. The visions show that he is a group person and I am a loner. My brother shares his energy with the others and I just simply go within myself and get it from the essence of my being."

"I was quite independent," continues Schenker. "I recorded *Lonesome Crow* when I was 15. I moved in with my girlfriend when I was 16. I told her, 'See those orange boxes over there? We can make some furniture out of them and we can move into a place.' She told her mother and she was like, 'No way!' She started buying us furniture. I remember being 16 years old and lying there talking to my girlfriend and I told her, 'You can drop me off in the middle of China and I would know what to do.' I always knew. When I was 16, I knew anything was possible. I told my girlfriend then, 'One day I am going to be one of the best guitarists in the world.' She just laughed."

"We don't talk about things like that," reflects Michael, asked if there was jealousy from Rudolf at how adept Michael was at lead guitar. "I think we respect each other. The way we grew up, there was no competition and no fights. For instance, I wouldn't go to my parents and ask for money; I would just earn it myself. We had a unique upbringing. At the same time, we are both very visual. In order to get somewhere in life, you need to have a vision. The vision brings you to the table. Without a vision, you just do what everybody else does and you are just there. If you are an individual then you create something unique; it's just the way it goes. My whole family are very emotional people. Everything created is created with a lot of feel."

"I think my development as musician was different than the usual," said Michael, speaking with Guitar 2001 magazine. "People like to become a musician because they get applause, and they get a lot of money and they get famous and all the attention. But I was just so fascinated with the sound of the guitar itself. I just got so involved with the sound in those six strings that I didn't see any other side of it. It was just the pure excitement about the sound and the idea I had of how I wanted to play it."

"Basically, it's a reflection of your own tastes," added Michael, specifically on the subject of soloing. "Whatever you want to do is what you become. If you want to be a flashy guitarist, you'll be a flashy guitarist. Unless you're trapped in a puppet-type situation where you *have to* make hit records. If you really do what you want to do, regardless if it makes a lot of money or not, you really end up where you want to end up. It's the choices we make. Like, what kind of sound you want, how you want to play. I knew what kind of sound I liked, how much vibrato, how much technique and how much melody—and all these mixed together to create my own style. Every person has something unique to offer if they look inside themselves, rather than externally. It's all about choices that we make, and that's who we are."

In a conversation with John Stix from Guitar for the Practising Musician, other details of Michael's formative years emerge. "I started learning Shadows songs when I was nine," begins Schenker. "Until I was 13, I learned whatever was on the radio, the Beatles, the Stones. Then it was Beck, Page, Clapton and Hendrix. The last thing I copied was Leslie West, when I was 16 or 17. That was it. From then on, I locked myself in a room and practised. Once I put all the albums away and started writing, recording and playing harmony parts, I realised that I had my own sense of taste and melody. I think it's the melody more than anything else that helps me stand out."

"I started playing the guitar because Rudolf asked me if I could figure out something for him. I said, 'I can't play.' He said, 'Just try it.' I switched on the tape recorder and tried to find the first note. Then I rewound it and made sure it fit. Before I knew it, I was able to play a whole instrumental album of the Shadows. At that time I wasn't thinking of live performance. I was having fun and I was absolutely amazed that it was possible for me to do this."

"The next step was when I was 11, and somebody was looking for a guitarist and my brother told me I should go there. 'But what is it all about?' I asked. He said, 'Go out on stage and play.' So that was the second step. When you're a young player and you have just started to take it seriously, you progress much faster. You see the progress much clearer than after a certain amount of years. Once you get better and better, progress become slower and slower in certain ways, unless your aim is to be one of the fastest guitar players in the world. That was not my aim. In fact, I used to say I had to cut down my practising because I was getting too fast."

"Eventually, in Germany, I was working much too hard, and everything else happened much too slow around me. That's why when I got the offer from UFO, I took it straight away. I was serious. If I put myself in a room for eight hours a day of practice, I didn't want somebody else messing around. I wanted to be in surroundings to expect the same from others, work as hard as a team. In Germany it was impossible. My brother was working very hard, but he was being manager and everything at the same time."

"Basically, we were still learning how to play," offers Pete, contrasting the pre-Schenker albums with *Phenomenon*. "And when *Phenomenon* came up, we had played quite a bit live because those records had sold reasonably well in places like France, Germany and Japan, so it gave us the opportunity to play concerts to quite a lot of people compared to other bands our age. We were really only like 17, 18 and we had gotten better. By the time Michael had come in we were able to develop along with Michael and his style of playing. We were really a band that was growing, developing a sound together."

"When Michael joined for *Phenomenon*, he was the lucky link," adds Phil. "It made our sound, which I think is very British, and a little bit European. With Michael in it, you can hear German or Teutonic notes or notations in his playing. So it became a very European rock band, second or third generation."

"It's just the people, the combination of Michael's writing and playing and the stuff that Pete and I come up with. Put them together and we have UFO. We've tried, we've had other combinations with different players, but it's never quite been the same. Michael comes up with this slightly German, dramatic European sound, while Pete's stuff is a cut between American rock 'n' roll and the English music of say, The Who and the Small Faces."

By this point, Michael had moved over to England and was sharing a flat with Phil in Palmers Green, North London, where Michael promptly rescued a rabbit next door that was being fattened up by the neighbour for slaughter and subsequent Christmas dinner. As Phil chuckles, Michael swore the rabbit would bring the band good luck, but in the meantime, all it did was defecate all over the apartment.

As an interesting side note, Michael ponders the question of the first UFO song he ever wrote. "With UFO? Well, I know that 'In Search of the Peace of Mind' was the first song I ever wrote, and that was on *Lonesome Crow*, by Scorpions. And then the first one with UFO might have been... there was like a single we released, which was called 'Give Her the Gun;' that could've been the first song."

The track Michael is referring to was a rollicking blues-tinged hard rocker that was released as a single in Germany in 1973, but not included on the *Phenomenon* album. On the B-side was yet another non-LP track, "Sweet Little Thing," which begins very much like future smash hit "Only You Can Rock Me," before collapsing into a dated, deflated, stodgy honky tonk boogie. Nonetheless, both songs were hard rock, and when added to consideration of the *Phenomenon* era, perhaps point to a more electric and guitar-ish future to come.

"Give Her the Gun" is critical in the UFO saga for another reason, as Leo Lyons, producer of the song, as well as the subsequent three UFO albums, *Phenomenon, Force It* and *No Heavy Petting*, explains. "Basically, Chrysalis were thinking of signing UFO and were looking for a producer and they had talked to me. I had not really produced anything commercially. They were interested in the band because they had sold some records in Germany. I had worked on development deals, particularly with Frankie Miller for Chrysalis, having recorded him at my home studio and they knew what my contribution was to Ten Years After."

"So they said to me, 'Well, we've got this band; we'll give you a day in the studio with them.' We went in the studio and we cut that track and I think maybe we did another one too, which was an instrumental. But that, if you like, was mine and UFO's audition piece for Chrysalis. That was in Chipping Norton Studios. I do remember that, because it was the first time I'd gone in. I went back the next day and paid my own money for two hours studio time to mix it, because of course, we had to record and mix it all at the same time." Lyons also has said that the band had to hop a ferry for an upcoming gig, and that Phil had subsequently called him from Dover asking if he was available to produce the band's next album.

Lyons' credits include his membership in Ten Years After as bassist and songwriter, as well as The Jaybirds and studio work before that. Through the years, there has been extensive production work (including Magnum, post-UFO outfit Waysted, Richard and Linda Thompson and Procol Harum) as well as engineering, a reformation of Ten Years After (including touring and both studio and live albums) plus songwriting for country artists in Nashville, where Leo currently resides.

"I think I worked in Morgan because I felt comfortable there," adds Leo, looking back at Morgan Studios, the recording locale for all three of his albums with the band. "Although, at the time of *No Heavy Petting*, I was managing Wessex Studios, and we did do some tracking at Wessex, which Queen used. Morgan was quite a hip studio or an 'in' studio at the time. Yes had recorded there, Rod Stewart, Tull, Ten Years After. It was probably the first eight-track and then 16-track in

London, although obviously everyone else caught up with it. Small studio, and I remember when I was doing an acoustic album there, you could actually hear the traffic noise. It was fairly primitive, but so were a lot of great studios at the time. There was a coffee shop, a little restaurant there, and everybody dropped in after hours whether they were recording or not."

Lyons had been given a budget of £1500 to make *Phenomenon*, Chrysalis having been pleased with the two tracks of demo recordings. The album was whipped together in ten days. Adding the following with respect to the band's curious chemistry, Leo says that, "The first record I did with them, Michael didn't even speak English. I used to be fairly fluent in German so that wasn't a problem for me. But I could see that he was getting frustrated with the other guys. And Pete and Phil were very relaxed; they had their own band sense of humour and here you've got a guy who doesn't speak English, that comes in on it. So yeah, I could see that there were a few problems. Phil always came in at the last minute with his lyrics, but then I like his lyrics. I like a lot of his singing; I thought he had a great voice. But they always came in last. I've probably been quoted before as saying that for most of the records I did, I was producing backing tracks and then hoping that we can fit the song on top. Being a songwriter myself, that's pretty frustrating."

Concerning Andy Parker, "Very much an underrated drummer. I listened to some UFO stuff about a month ago and I thought well, golly, this guy was really good. Andy was his own man. He came in, played the drums and left. The beginning and the end. Pete and Phil were the two guys who had been together forever and they were the guys you worked with, often making Andy the butt of their jokes. Schenker was the new man. But as a rhythm section, Pete and Andy worked well together."

As the "new man" as Leo puts it, Michael definitely put up with a lot of mental terrorism from the tight-knit group of English lads. "Well, Phil used to be a fighter and there was a lot of sarcasm and a lot of button-pushing-type stuff going on, based on mental development," says Schenker. "Now they're a little more focused on the music itself, rather than being a nuisance (laughs). I guess UFO is a chemistry that is not based on time, it's based on who we are and what we do."

Working with Leo was future production legend Chris Tsangarides. "He was actually the assistant engineer on *Phenomenon*," confirms

Parker. "It was like his first major gig, I think, in the business. About 17 or something. Yeah, he had like a big mop of curly hair. But he doesn't have that anymore. I had a big mop of curly hair then too (laughs). Back then, assistant engineer was everything from making the tea, sweeping the floors, and then they had to stick those huge reels of tape on the machine and then do some of the editing. Because it was funny, we were talking about how his razor blades always used to go missing back in those days. 'Yeah, especially when you guys were in there. You could never find a razor blade' (laughs). But those days have passed, you know."

"I had just started at the studio," recalls Tsangarides. "I was about 18 years old. Up to that point I'd be going to gigs all over the place in London, and I was well into that, and I would be seeing UFO playing at the Greyhound in Fulham which is a pub, and Priest playing at Slough Technical College. I think a lot of it was we had Sabbath that were hitting big, and there all of a sudden the likes of Jethro Tull and Queen was starting to do something, and Priest were kind of following off from that sort of tradition."

"But UFO, there is none more melodic than Michael Schenker on guitar," continues Chris. "Their songs that they wrote were very melodic, although hard. But they were of the slower groove, I suppose, and if it was, if you want to call it anything, hard rock. It wasn't doomy things or whatever. Later there were keyboards, which was basically a Hammond organ and the piano. So that gave it a different sort of edge. Mogg's voice was not always particularly high-pitched; if he was singing a different style of music it would be crooning, you know (laughs). So it had that real lovely melody, and the guitars that Michael would play, and the keyboards in there—it was great. I mean, I was the tape-op on their albums, back in the day, so I saw firsthand what they did. It was fantastic. The producer was Leo Lyons of Ten Years After, of that ilk. Very well-regarded, definitely. A big influence on Iron Maiden, Steve Harris, was the band Stray, who began around '68, I believe, but another one was UFO. Steve's whole thing, his suit, was what Pete Way used to wear, and running around like he did. Maiden came from that school."

Visually, *Phenomenon* would mark the beginning of a fruitful working relationship. "*Phenomenon* had that album cover I loved, and that got us involved with Hipgnosis," recalls Phil, with respect to the surreal and legendary graphics house most famous for their work with Pink Floyd. "There aren't a lot they did that I actually don't like. They were all kind of different and interesting to do. The people we worked with were either quite fun or bizarre."

The record company bio issued to press with *Phenomenon* opened with a salvo about the association with Hipgnosis, writing, "Many journalists, media gurus and people in the rock biz who know about such things rated the cover art on UFO's *Phenomenon* the top sleeve graphics of 1974. Hipgnosis' intriguing picture-within-a-picture view of a flying saucer hoax proved merely the appetizer of the package though. The stomping main course lay within, provoking a wild range of comparisons, with one Los Angeles disc jockey even dubbing UFO, 'the English Steely Dan.' Group leader/vocalist Phil Mogg can't quite agree with the Dan reference, but he will admit *Phenomenon* put his quartet on the map in previously alien territory, Britain and the US. The curious state of affairs prior to the LP had the band's success confined to loyal outposts in Europe and Japan."

Storm Thorgerson and Aubrey Powell from Hipgnosis, for their part, considered the hand-tinting process used for the *Phenomenon* image as "expressionistic" as opposed to "impressionistic," aligning it with what they did for Led Zeppelin on *Houses of the Holy*. They also found the process of "accentuating the expected natural colours" to be painstaking, one that could easily result in the artwork being turned into the label late. As is the graphic house's oeuvre, the shot plays up goings-on in suburbia. Hipgnosis proceed to inject sarcasm into UFO's chosen title for the record, with a picture depicting a man tossing a hubcap in the air (note the tyre iron next to the driver's side front wheel) while his wife gets the shot, herself and her guilt captured by a second shooter.

Musically, *Phenomenon*, issued May 1974, would turn out to be a record of nice enough experiments, penetrated forcefully by two of the band's all-time classics in "Doctor Doctor" and "Rock Bottom," quite the phenomenon in and of itself, this idea that what is essentially a "debut" record could cough up not one but two larger than life anthems. "Good question," laughs Leo, when asked why the lay of the land was this way—two modern metal classics in a sea of what was mostly acoustic pondering. "I guess it's just the material that the band had. They had a few basic ideas put together and we went in the studio and worked around them. I mean, Schenker is a melodic guitar player; he certainly was then and I guess it just turned out that way. I may have encouraged it, I don't know."

But across the landscape of *Phenomenon*, polite modesty and amusing curio reigned. Opener "Too Young to Know" is a clean and disciplined cross between pop and glam, evoking the sounds of Mott the Hoople and David Bowie, although the biggest surprise is how much better the band instantly sounded versus the bulldozing primary colours of the early three records, with Phil's lyric speaking of the cad corrupting an innocent young girl. "Crystal Light" followed in a cozy, gauzy folk direction, Phil turning in a good early lyric concerning hitting the open road, in the cold, moon above, his imagery near visceral.

Then it's time for UFO 2.0 to explode from the grooves, middle of side one, introducing their new guitarist to the masses. "Doctor Doctor" instantly established Schenker as a guitar god, even though in studio form, the song is quite an understated entity. Nonetheless there's a mournful quality to the riff, as well as a twin lead solo that is characteristically, for Michael, musical, memorable, without flash. Oddly, the track would have fit more comfortably on Scorpions' *In Trance*, *Virgin Killer* or *Taken by Force*, as written by Uli Roth rather than Michael's brother, Rudolf. Put differently, the song is extremely German, perhaps the most "ethnic" thing Michael would ever bring to UFO's alcohol-soaked table.

"That was one of the very first things we did, I think," says Pete, of the track. "When it first came out in Europe, I think it sold about ten copies as a single. When we came back with *Strangers in the Night*, when that record became big, suddenly all the songs we'd been doing for a long time became very popular. 'Doctor Doctor' became very much an anthem and it still is. I mean, it already was popular, for the 2,000 or 3,000 people who would come see us every night. But it wasn't until *Strangers*, when we were playing the bigger places in America... for instance, in Chicago, I think there were about 14,000 at that show. It's that type of song that gets them going; it's an audience song. So it's funny, it was a rediscovered song, but it was always popular. I'll tell you what. You do festivals and stuff, which we were recently doing in Europe, and let me assure you, you play 'Doctor Doctor' and suddenly the whole festival... you've got 40,000 people jumping up and down going 'Doctor, doctor, please!' You know, I'm not saying that it's something we save to make our performance go down well. But you've got the other side of the coin where unless we do it, people go, 'They didn't play "Doctor Doctor".'

Phil's lyric doesn't say much—it's only few words, and many of those repetitious—but what it does say paints an amusing picture of the narrator needing a doctor's patching-up skills after a love goes wrong and metaphorically life-threatening. Over time, given the often dire drug-strewn history of the band, the lyric has by osmosis come to represent the idea of calling for rescue from addiction (the evil temptress in the song might be cocaine), or even the idea of calling for the same type of rock doc requested by Ozzy in "Rock 'n' Roll Doctor," namely a physician who doesn't mind reaching into his black bag for—or writing a prescription for—drugs requested from more of a recreational point of view. The song was issued as a single at the time but failed to chart, even though, as Pete alluded to, up into 1979, UFO would have themselves a considerable hit with a live version of the track from the *Strangers in the Night* album, "Doctor Doctor" reaching No.35 on the charts.

"I can tell you the procedure, the process that I was using," adds Michael. "I was actually playing with a Echoplex in those days, like an echo loop—it would go around. You would play a little something and then it would keep coming back, and then you could play something else to it and it would kind of turn into three-part harmony and stuff like that. So that's how I started off 'Doctor Doctor.' Then I gave it to Phil and then he was singing to it, and then we added some stuff to it for the vocals. He came over and we worked on that and that was basically it. So yes, I had this riff, and I remember Phil coming over saying, 'Play this part again, play this part again' and then back and forth and we finally had it."

"I think in lead guitar, basically," explains Michael, further offering a glimpse into his methodology. "When I want to write an album, I can't really look too much at the individual songs for some reason. It's different for me. It's like I'm more into this world of improvisation and lead guitar (laughs). It's a bit like I write a song and then I go on a separate journey. It's like an entry or entrance into an adventure. The entrance to the adventure is the music and the guitar solo and then there is an end to that part, and the adventure is then the rest of the song. That's how I feel. So when I make a record, I don't really individualize the songs so much. I kind of look at the whole album as one flow. It's kind of weird but that's what I do. So people start talking about a particular song and it's difficult for me to comment. You hear people mention a particular song, and it seems to the same ones mentioned over and over and over, like for instance 'Doctor Doctor' or 'Rock Bottom.' These are the ones people worldwide agree on, that these are the favourite songs. But the song itself is not something I focus on when I wrote them, but it's great to know that they have left an impression on people."

"We were like, (in camp voice), 'We've got to have that boy! Got to have him!'" jokes Phil, in conversation with Tim Jones, on acquiring Michael and then writing this signature track. "We were on our way—so we thought! We wrote as best we could, but due to Michael's English, 'Doctor Doctor' was taking forever. Then one day it came. I get snippets in bed and have to write it down or you forget, especially if you suffer from boozeheimer's disease (laughs)."

Phil Mogg elaborates on UFO's writing process. "Well yes, we need a correction here. It's often, 'You give me guitar chords and I'll put the rest on.' So that includes humming a tune, the melody and the writing. There's a whole schmear after 'You play me three chords and I'll put the rest on.' That's where it goes. In actual fact, it's a whole fucking task. But basically I couldn't do my bit without the bottom bit. If somebody didn't come up and play A, G and E, I couldn't do the next step, and it was always a group thing anyway. But we were lazy fuckers. Always do the minimal amount and that's it. There's nothing left over."

"Very interesting for me as a bass player, actually," adds Pete Way, in conversation with Rich Davenport, on the subject of writing with Michael. "In those days, you know, a guitar player would expect his bass player to go berserk on the bass, like in the days of The Cream. When I started working with Michael, he just wanted me to *not* play, really. Because that competed with his guitar melodies and I wasn't breaking them down by overplaying. So it actually made my job easy. It's funny, 'Prince Kajuku' we even played with Michael; Michael used to like it. It's a bit like Mozart telling you that, you know, knocking down a brick wall is quite a good sound or whatever. I told him how to do it, and whether he got the message, you know, he played a good solo. Because we did it with Mick, obviously, and Michael just went, 'Oh, I know this song; it's good.' Michael knew it because he's younger than us and when he grew up, he heard it on German radio."

Back to the record, "Space Child," another forgotten bit of crumpet and one of fully seven songs on the album credited to Michael and Phil alone, came next. The song is a dark, dreamy acoustic number one could imagine on, say, the debut Rainbow album. But closing side one is the album's second and last, lasting contribution, namely "Rock Bottom," an uncompromisingly heavy rocker strapped to a rocket of a riff. Phil's lyrics cryptically address aging and death (he claims some inspiration from a horror film), but mostly just the age-old concept of corruption, an idea that is at the heart of most of Mogg's morality plays, and indeed, in all its strata, at the heart of all of living.

"'Rock Bottom' is a good one," muses Michael. "We were all in the rehearsal studio and Phil was reading the paper and we were just desperately trying to find something really good. So we were all jamming, jamming, jamming and then I started that riff, 'Rock Bottom,' and then Phil jumped up and yelled 'That's it!' Funny. But writing in general, there's not too much to it. Writing songs, I'm just being myself. I practice and that's when I find something to work on. Usually the songs that I write are all by accident. When I practice, I bump into something I like and I put it on a cassette. They are usually ten seconds of pieces, and then when it's time to make the record, I listen to those pieces and whatever inspires me most, I take that and turn it into songs. Then when I finish the instrumental parts, I give that part to the singer and then he does the rest. So it's not really so much like, 'I met this girl and I wanted to write a song about her' or something like that. Everything I do, it's really all musical."

Over the years, Michael has repeatedly expressed his fondness for "Rock Bottom," notably for its jammy middle section inside of which he's been able to play free form and have this extended solo section evolve dramatically through time, through his original tenure with UFO and back in and then permanently out of the band over the decades, the track having been firmly lodged in his solo over the course of the 2000s.

Onto side two and nothing much lasted, even if "Oh My" was a solid boogie-ish hard rocker that might have given Quo a run for its money back in the day. The song lived for a while live, and it's in fact a consummate pub rockin' track, Phil turning in a lyric all about bravado, making a splash. Willie Dixon cover "Built for Comfort" hung around for a while, marrying this version of the band to the yobbish, hard-hitting blues band UFO once was. Phil has said that the song was chosen from a four-track EP the band had found that included "Smokestack Lightning," and that doing "Built for Comfort" demonstrated Michael's versatility, even if no one saw Schenker as much of a blues guy.

"Time On My Hands" is another of the record's perfectly serviceable folk songs, something that Free or Humble Pie might do during reflective moments. "Lipstick Traces" was the B-side to the "Doctor Doctor" single, the spot of product actually emerging two months before the full album. It's an acoustic number penned by Schenker, a track reminiscent of similar desperado-like excursions Thin Lizzy would go on in the pre-*Fighting* years.

"When people ask me my favourite song," said Michael, back in 1988, "I always go back to 'Lipstick Traces' on the first UFO album. It was the first great instrumental I'd ever written. It gave many people goose bumps. It's special because I was so young when I wrote it. I think that's how I started getting into romantic instrumentals."

The album closes with "Queen of the Deep," which reminds this writer of Budgie. The song is dark and ponderous and mixes murky acoustic passages with even murkier heavy chording and riffing.

To reiterate, the sum total of *Phenomenon* is virtually forgotten but for ardent students of UFO, save for the two monster sledges seared into the hard rock history books. But as well, the totality of the album is anything but forgettable. Fact is, the band had written a solid and varied collection of songs that was professional, brave, not particularly dated, and far from the juvenilia of *1* and *Flying*. Fortunately for us as listeners and for them as a band, UFO did not rest on their laurels, moving forward quickly and forcefully toward a follow-up record with their new German axeman.

The 2007 CD reissue of *Phenomenon* included the aforementioned "Give Her the Gun," along with both demo and finished versions of a band original called "Sixteen." Essentially written no further than a middling Kiss song, "Sixteen" is dated hard rock crossing into funk and the type of predictable heavy riffing one hears just this side of the British blues boom. There's also a demo version of "Oh My," a live version of "Doctor Doctor" and the B-side to the "Give Her the Gun" single, namely "Sweet Little Thing." This one is like "Sixteen" but even more bar-room rocking and amateurish, almost as rudimentary as the material across the Bolton albums. The demos of "Oh My" and "Sixteen" feature Bernie Marsden on guitar and not Schenker.

Amusingly, Rolling Stone, given their well-documented anti-hard rock bias over the years, ran a very positive review of *Phenomenon*,

Gordon Fletcher calling the band legendary, predicting big things for them swiftly. Fletcher called the album "one of the most exciting debuts of the year," debut in that *Phenomenon* was the first UFO album with widespread US release. Fletcher further deemed it "an artfully controlled disc lit with furious bits of creative energy." Fletcher went on to compare Schenker to Jimmy Page, calling him the band's "focal point, with incisive and exciting playing that's guaranteed to make people sit up and take notice." After more eloquent and effusive words, particularly for "Rock Bottom" and "Oh My," he calls the album cover "one of the year's best." Billboard was equally pleased, calling each and every track a potential single.

"Don't listen to the first two tracks on this album," warned P.M. from influential English weekly Sounds. "They're awful. But if you do hear them, don't let it put you off the album because it's quite good and shows promising flickers of what the band could develop into. This band have changed quite a few times since they were 'the first band to break in Japan.' What can I say about them? They're just a tight, little heavy rock unit. It's so boring writing about rock groups because you keep having to repeat your superlatives like 'terrif' and 'amazing' but that's neither here nor there. There's touches of Sabbath, Zep, Budgie and Free in their music. But listen to 'Space Child,' 'Rock Bottom' and 'Time on My Hands,' they're pretty ama... oh dorks, there I go again."

Melody Maker was less complimentary, J.W. writing that, "When you're told, the band has a 'strong continental reputation,' you are liable to experience a cynical recoil—the 'big on the continent' syndrome doesn't cut much ice. *Phenomenon* is their first album for Chrysalis, but phenomenon it most certainly is not. It's slim pickings, and mostly a vehicle for the ravings of guitarist Michael Schenker. There's nothing on this album that hasn't been said (better and worse) many times before. It's tight but tiresome. However, the record is not really representative of UFO as they are now because it was apparently recorded before they augmented another guitarist into their line-up: Paul Chapman, formerly of Skid Row. But with their new man, they'll have to come up with something a lot more original than the present offering."

As the piece stated, touring for *Phenomenon* included Welshman Paul Chapman in the ranks. Paul would of course figure prominently beginning with the tour for the smash *Strangers in the Night* album, through four fine albums in the early '80s.

Says Chapman, "When they did *Phenomenon*, before they went out on the road to support it, they needed another guitar player. Well, I had just left a band called Skid Row which was a three-piece Irish band. I took Gary Moore's place in Skid Row, when I was 16. I played with them for almost two years, '71, '72, and Pete and Phil had apparently seen me play in Skid Row, at the Marquee Club. I had been disgruntled with Skid Row because I thought everybody was lazy (laughs). So I hitchhiked to London and stayed with a friend and had answered an ad in Melody Maker. And when I phoned for the audition, I apparently—well, Phil Campbell (Persian Risk, Motörhead) told me just in the last few years—that I actually had the gig before I even went there because I was the only person who called up that had some kind of reputation."

Chapman, from Cardiff had joined Skid Row in December 1971, having arrived at that point out of his hometown band, Universe, lasting with the Irish outfit until July '72. The next couple of years had been spent with a band called Kimla Taz, at which point he spotted the ad in Melody Maker placed there by UFO, looking for a second guitarist. Subsequently Paul auditioned, at the Unity Theatre in London, and scored the gig, although as he states, it looks like he was a shoe-in anyway.

"And when I got the gig I said, 'Look, I've been in a three-piece band and it was hellfire.' With a three-piece band, there's lots of guitar, of course. There's no way I'm going to be a rhythm guitar player. I was used to being the main guitar player. So we decided to split the guitar stuff 50/50 with Michael and I down the middle. So I was in the band with Michael for about nine months to a year, beginning in April '73 I guess, and we were writing the next album, which turned into *Force It*. Well anyway, I left and formed Lone Star at that point, and got that rolling, and lo and behold, a lot of the ideas I had for Lone Star are in the UFO stuff as well (laughs)."

Paul has said that part of the reason he had left had to do with his Welsh sensibilities versus the London style of both Pete and Phil, perhaps a bit of homesickness entering the brew as well, given that he had been in London for two years with the transplanted Skid Row. Creatively, Paul also has said that he had wanted a freer, less structured, more hippie-ish vibe to the music, citing Welsh homeland favourites Man as an example.

"Mick was actually my guitar tech," says Paul of Mick Bolton, guitarist of record for the three pre-Schenker UFO albums. "He came to work for the band. Phil was married to his sister, Anita. I kind of felt sorry for Mick because he shouldn't have been in that position. He was on the dole and he didn't have a job. So he came out, 'Oh, couldn't he be your guitar roadie?' 'Yeah!' But his soul wasn't in it. He really wasn't a roadie; he was a guitar player and it was a drag to have to go 'round the pub and drag him out of the pub to set up gear and stuff like that (laughs). Because he was more like a friend as opposed to somebody who works for you on a professional basis, you know what I mean? But no, I never did play with him. So yes, first it was Mick, then Larry Wallis, and then Bernie Marsden fits in before Michael."

Chapman goes on to offer insight into Michael's almost instantly strange position within the band. "Well, in the 1973/1974 period when it was a twin-guitar band, I used to room with Michael. Phil and Pete had a room, and then there was me and Michael and Andy; the drummer and the guitar players would kind of stick together like glue, so we could play. We used to play in hotels and it made sense for us to room together. Michael at that point... put it like this, when he joined the band he couldn't speak English, so at this point he's kind of learning English. So there's lots of peer pressure. Phil and Pete and Andy grew up together and there's a little pact there, being from London. I'm from Wales and I've never met these guys in my life, so Michael and I are kind of like outsiders that room together—he's German and I'm Welsh, and he can't speak English. So there's kind of like gang warfare. It was like cliques, and Michael was sensitive to that kind of thing. I'm a lot more thick-skinned myself; it doesn't make a difference to me. Fuck 'em, I don't care what they fucking say, to be honest. When I'm with Phil and Pete, everybody is ragging on Andy and when I'm with Phil and Andy, everyone is ragging on Pete. That's just how it is, very complicated."

"Well, I stayed with Michael and his girlfriend in London during that period, and Michael was showing signs of religious leanings. He used to have this little room that he made in his bedroom out of two shower curtains and a chair and a picture of Krishna, and I used to have to go in there to use their bathroom after Gaby had gone to work. He would be in there meditating. I would be like, 'Come on, do this; we've got to be at so-and-so by 11:00,' and he was like, 'Shhh, I've got to do this; I must do it for my sanity.' And then when we started touring Europe, we started getting alcohol on the rider and things like that tend to get magnified or amplified. At that point I left the band."

UFO indeed would end up all over Britain and Europe (Michael cites a Suzi Quatro jaunt as possibly the band's first tour), recording a few BBC appearances in their wake. An American tour was also mounted, in support of Steppenwolf, the band also showing up on Don Kirshner's Rock Concert, which, in the '70s, shared status with The Midnight Special as the only game in town for live hard rock on TV.

Paul Chapman would be out of the band by January '75, "Tonka," as he was called (named for the indestructible toy trucks), proving to be unreliable at this young age, too drunken for UFO if you can believe it, and missing a gig. He can be seen in many photos however, and heard on *BBC – In Session and Live*. Paul would resurface for two major label albums in Lone Star, before landing right back in UFO at the turn of the decade.

"When I left and went back to Wales, I said I was sick of it," reflects Chapman, offering a somewhat contradictory view to the above depiction of those days. "I'm sick of being in a band where everybody is taking the piss. I mean, Pete and Phil and Andy were from London, and Michael and myself were outsiders in this whole thing. It was kind of weird but I never felt uncomfortable in the whole thing. We just had different backgrounds and everything. So when I formed Lone Star, May of '75 or so, I said, if I'm going to do this, I really want to do it in a way, that, first off, it should be like the camaraderie you have on a rugby team. But also the players have to be incredibly good. That's the main part about it, and they have to be the right people from a personality point of view. They have to think professionally. Going back in the '70s, mid-'70s, everybody wanted to be... people like used car salesmen were still managing bands from like the '60s, and you had to try to think professionally and we did not want to be a local band. We wanted to take this and get a deal. So the first thing was, we had to have the right people, then we had to have the right planning, and then the right material and the right everything."

Says future UFO member Paul Raymond, reflecting on the situation decades later, "It didn't really work to have two guitar players at the same time all the time because Michael's style is so... you know, when you've got two really good lead guitar players, it was like those fucking solos... It was actually quite exciting, but it didn't work because

Michael's the lead player on the albums, so the solos were all Michael's. It's difficult to ask someone who can play really well solo-wise to just play rhythm, you know?"

If things went another route back in '74, Michael might have ended up "feeling the flow" of a very different sort than described above. "I got a phone call from someone who asked me if I wanted to audition for the Rolling Stones. I said, 'Wait a minute. I will let you know.' I hung up and I called up my brother and talked to him about it. Basically, what it came down to was that the step I took to join UFO was a big enough step for me to take. I was still only 17 years old. It was maybe even too big a step for me to fully digest. The image I grew up with of the Rolling Stones was drugs. Brian Jones had died. I called my brother because I was scared. I was attracted to it but I had my doubts about it. I asked my brother and I don't remember the exact conversation, but based on his feedback, I decided not to call back."

Chapter Five
Force It

"I want my guitar to sound like a finger with no bone"

UFO came back hard and heavy for *Force It*, an album issued with another amusing Hipgnosis wrapper, in July 1975. Quips Phil on the salacious sleeve, "They didn't want to see the nipple that was on European one, so in the American one they faded out the couple in the bath, because they thought it was offensive. I thought is was a bit strange because it wasn't anything too sexual, but they decided to fade the couple out, which kind of didn't really make a lot of sense for the cover then (laughs)."

The title of the album, *Force It*, contains the obvious sexual connotation, but it is also, in conjunction with the cover art, a play on the word faucet. The couple in the shower are none other that Genesis P-Orridge and his girlfriend Cosey Fanni Tutti, both from industrial noise terrorists Throbbing Gristle formed the following year. Because the focus wouldn't hold front to back on the set Hipnosis had constructed, at great cost, for the shoot, Storm and Aubrey had to take separate pictures of the various bits of plumbing hardware they had installed, and cut them into the foreground using their usual paste-up techniques.

"The guys that did those Pink Floyd albums," chuckles Pete, "they did some historic album covers, so we were lucky to use them or should I say get to work with them. When you work with people who've worked with the Floyd and Led Zeppelin, some really big people, you don't really question it. When they were shooting the pictures and ideas for it you might have thought it was a bit wild, but it always came out right—they're now classic covers."

"They wouldn't print it is America," confirms Andy. "I don't know if you've seen the difference in the European and the American one. That's all down to K-Mart, that American cover, because Chrysalis came to us and said, 'You know, K-Mart won't stock this album with that cover on it. If you want to sell them, they need to be...' That was before Wal-Mart got huge; it was with K-Mart, so we had to go with a steamed-out, watered-down version in order for K-Mart to stock it. It was the right decision because obviously that was about the only place kids could buy records—like Wal-Mart today. Small record shops are gone. But that was just something that Hipgnosis came up with. They were just amazing, those guys, Powell and Storm. They always came up with something spectacular. They just chucked us ideas and you'd go, 'Yeah, I like it.' I don't remember them giving us an idea that we didn't like, to be honest. They seemed to be in tune with us and the direction we were going; the covers just spoke volumes."

"I think it's innovative, it's raw," remarks Pete, on this first truly "realised" UFO album. "And it's interesting, because it's not one that Ron Nevison did; rather it was Leo Lyons. I think it's the work of a band who, once again, had been playing a lot, mainly in Europe, but of course in the states as well. I think it got to the Top 50 in America, thereabouts (actually No.71), to everybody's surprise. But it's a good album, lots of good riffs, great lead guitar, a real ballsiness, that thing you get when you play live and then you take that atmosphere into the rehearsal room."

Comparing the current producer and incoming Nevison, there for the big albums of the Schenker era, Way figures, "The difference between Leo and Ron was the fact that Leo was prepared to let long solos go on and things like that, because with Ten Years After, that's what they did. So it was very much a guitar thing. Ron brought bigger production into it, which later became that classic rock thing, AOR. But Leo, he was a good person to work with at that time because he let the band be the band. In terms of our sound, I'd say it's because our songs were quite commercial in a way, but rock. I think that was one of the keys to the band. We didn't sell out, but we managed to do songs that were still appreciated for the music and the melodies as much as they were for the hard, grinding guitars. But I really like *Force It*. I think out of all of those, *Force It* was a really cool one. They're all a bit like stepping stones, from the first one, which was, you know, okay, to the next one and the next one and the next one. Then we got to *Lights Out*, where we finally got our footing."

"I wasn't really focusing on him," says Michael on producer Leo Lyons. "I was focusing on my guitar playing and what I wanted. He was just a person there who was directing, coordinating the process of it. I don't think he did much other than coordinating, because when it came down to sound and stuff like that, I more or less directed to the engineer what I wanted etc. If someone like Ron Nevison would have done the first three albums it would've been a different picture. But anyway, it was a start for us and he was with Chrysalis. I guess because he wanted to get into the producing area, Chrysalis suggested UFO, so we got together. He had some strange approaches like turning down, playing really quiet and very clean and all of that. It sometimes disturbed me a little (laughs), so I had to fight pretty hard to get to the point of distortion. Because I knew exactly what I wanted. I had to describe to him the sound I wanted. With my little bit of English, it was pretty hard, but I managed. I would explain to him, I want my guitar to sound like a finger with no bone (laughs)."

"I doubt that that would be Michael's thing," laughs Leo, finding this whole "turning down" comment from Michael baffling. "I wouldn't think so, no. I don't think I made him play really quietly. I mean, there were limitations as to how loud we could play when we were tracking because of the studio, but maybe it was really, really quiet for Michael; I don't know. But not intentionally, no."

I asked Michael if he felt that he had made considerable improvements by the time of *Force It*. "Well, in those years, you developed very fast. So from album to album there is an improvement. When I listen to it, from a technical point of view, the vibrato improved, you know, different things just improved. The longer you play, the more you develop your skills. I'm still playing 'Let It Roll.' But it's very hard for me to do that stuff because what happens, when I do music, I'm in the moment. Whenever I do it, I'm totally behind it, because I only do what I really like."

"So different reasons, in different songs; for me, the music, the solo parts, stuff like that, is for me the highlight. Rather than if the song is good or not. If I play a really good solo I like... how can I say this? It's for me an adventure, when I'm creating, because I'm going deep inside myself. It comes from a well that is infinite, and depending on how deep I go, certain things come out. And it's usually pretty deep. The rest really comes down to taste. Some people like this one, other people can identify more with the other one and so on. When we put the set together, with five people in the band, we've got five different sets. So to discuss... like I said, I view music totally different from what the consumer does. Because I'm connected on a whole different level, so it's usually very hard to understand where I'm coming from. But what the result is, is really based on the differences between people's tastes."

"Let It Roll" is indeed, worth playing after all these years, and it's no surprise that it's in UFO's set to this day as well. "Let It Roll" is one of the early galloping speed metal songs, marking a fresh, more technical type of hard rock, Phil turning in a naff lyric somewhat concerned with racing. In terms of the gallop, well, UFO was already pioneering this form with "Doctor Doctor," even if that was more of a mid-paced vibe.

Although Paul Chapman says that "'Let It Roll' and 'Mother Mary,' which I should have got credit on, were written when I was in the band between *Phenomenon* and *Force It*," Pete says, more so referring the credit angle, that, "No, that's not correct at all. Not as far as I know; not to my memory. But you know, certain people think certain things. Actually, the only thing I think Paul was involved with was 'Shoot Shoot.' But let me assure you, he was nowhere near 'Let It Roll' or anything like that. He does have dreams of stardom."

"Let It Roll" is driven by a heck of a performance from Andy Parker. Turns out it was a rare instance of the UFO percussionist using double bass drum, Andy somewhat passing by the idea randomly the way Nicko McBrain has in Maiden, namely a couple times across the expanse of a massive catalogue.

"I was a huge Jimi Hendrix fan and a huge Cream fan," begins Parker, as background. "Ginger Baker is one of my all-time influences drum-wise; I loved the way that guy played and still do. I recently saw that concert that they did, the Albert Hall concerts when Cream reformed. I saw it on TV and man, he still plays as good as ever, don't he? So a massive influence on me, plus Hendrix. I had a huge purple and green poster of Hendrix on my bedroom wall for years; I just worshipped the guy."

"But Ginger was one of the first guys I saw using two kicks, which opened a new door for me. I thought, man I gotta try this! Because that was before they'd been to the double pedal for one bass drum—it's a lot easier than carrying another bass drum around. Why someone didn't come out with it sooner... I mean, I've always loved the look of it anyway. I just loved the symmetry with the two kicks and I still use them today. But yeah Ginger used them a lot. Jon Hiseman with Colosseum and Tempest was another guy with two bass drums. There was a guy called Eric Delaney who was a well-known British drummer who used two kicks. But Ginger was heavy, fat and heavy, especially the solo on Blind Faith's album, 'Do What You Like'—that's got some great stuff in there with the two kicks. It's just for me, you know, hey this is new, and it's cool when you've got like just bass and drums to keep things going when somebody's soloing. I can be filling the bottom in a little more; you can put the extra kick in there to give it a bit more umph."

"So yeah, I used it—and use it live—mostly in 'Let It Roll.' Also 'I'm a Loser.' And barely at all any more, so mostly old stuff. I don't use it as much as some, to be honest. But I have two kicks on stage now. I don't think I had it on *Phenomenon*; I think maybe *Force It* is when I started using two bass drums. I'd put it in a bridge or something, as we changed the set-up sometimes. You'd think, oh man all my good double kicks are going, and it's like you chucked them out. I have to try and come up with a few newer ones. When I came back on and did *Monkey Puzzle*, the material was pretty much written and there just didn't seem to be a place for it in there. We've gone a bit bluesy and a bit different. Live I use it in certain fills, but like I said, 'Let It Roll' is a total double kick thing all the way through. Come to think of it, *Strangers in the Night* has quite a lot of it."

"With *Force It*, I guess it was just the way we were progressing," continues Parker. "Like I said, I got the two kicks then so that made a difference for me. This is our second album with Leo who's actually... I was a lot more comfortable with him, having done *Phenomenon* with him, which was a pretty successful album for us. But it's just the way you progress. Obviously Michael had been in it longer then and we were finding our way. You know how things develop when you put musicians together. The longer they're together, you start to feed off of each other, and I think it was just a natural progression for us to get heavier. I don't think it was anything where we thought, 'Oh we need to make a heavier album.' We've never been that kind of band. It's just the way people were writing, influences, what you were listening to at the time and then what you come up with. I don't think there was anything magical in there. We got more into keyboards. Chick Churchill did some guest keyboards on *Force It*."

"Shoot Shoot" is another classic and concert mainstay from *Force It*, with its pulsating accessible hard rock verve and subsequent validation as a bit of a life-sustaining hit. Phil, quite economically, paints a picture of murder for love, the twist in the tale being betrayal. Phil's inspiration was a girlfriend from Texas who was the first he ever knew who had her own gun. "Shoot Shoot" was issued as a single, but only in Germany and Austria, backed with album track "Love Lost Love."

"High Flyer" comes next, the band offering a morose acoustic ballad that would have fit cosily on *Phenomenon*. Thematically, pair this one with the much more successful, less oblique lyric that Phil would pen eight years hence for "Dreaming." "High Flyer" was the record's second and last single, backed with "Let It Roll." Next up was the aforementioned "Love Lost Love," a chunky, funky, bright hard rocker—if anything on *Force It* can be considered bright, due to the album's very drab, midrange-rife production values. Again, as Phil would bring forth on "Dreaming" from 1982's *Mechanix*, there's this idea of yearning desperately to make it in rock 'n' roll.

Closing out side two is a second tier UFO classic called "Out in the Streets," a song that demonstrates the band's deft control of dynamics, as well as skilled use of keyboards, on this particular album, as mentioned by Andy, provided by Ten Years After's chain-smoking Chick Churchill, at band mate Leo Lyons' suggestion. Phil's lyric evokes the glory of the vaudeville years, including mention of Buster Keaton and Louise Fazenda, an actress with 134 movies to her name from 1913 to 1935.

"'Out in the Streets' was almost like a folk song I was doing on bass," recalls Pete. "I can't remember the name of the song, but I think The Byrds did it. Me, I always put aggressive things in, but I kind of like melodies too. Sometimes I sit for hours... I don't particularly enjoy playing bass guitar, but I enjoy playing bass guitar with people I enjoy doing it with. So that used to give me inspiration. We used to go around the pub, come back, plug in and bang away, and if somebody had a riff, you'd joined in. Phil would go 'Let it roll, let it roll' or whatever. It was very spontaneous to a certain extent. It might have been something you've been practicing at home for ages and you go,

'I just want to play the riff for the boys.' But you'd go around the pub, come back and then you'd pick it up, all of us. It was very spontaneous. I would like to say that writing songs in the studio and presenting it to the band is great, but sometimes spontaneity really works."

Asked if there was any thought of keeping Chick on as a permanent member of the band, Way says, "Not really; it's odd actually. We counted him as older than us. We were just like four juvenile delinquents, me and Michael and Phil and Andy. So we were a four-piece band but we were writing songs that had a reason to have keyboards."

"Yes, there was; they did think about that," counters Gary Lyons. "But I think Chick blew it, in as much as he didn't really fit into it personality-wise with the rest of the guys. I mean, I don't know, you'd have to ask them that. But he did join them briefly and I think he did rehearse with them."

Onto side two and "Mother Mary" bursts through the door with a sinister metal riff plus an innovative and geometrical descending pattern come chorus time, courtesy of Paul Chapman, who despite Pete's protests, has proof of his creative contribution, namely Lone Star demos.

"Yeah, I had the songs before going into the band. It was a bit like how it works for the Lone Star stuff. It was like a hangover thing. In actual fact, if you listen to 'Mother Mary,' we were writing *Force It* when I went back down to Wales and started to form Lone Star. I just didn't go back to London. I called up and they were in America or Germany or something and I went, 'Oh well.' But I had the other thing kinda started. If you listen on the second Lone Star album, there's a track called 'From All of Us to All of You,' and there's a middle part that goes (sings it) and it's exactly the same part as on 'Mother Mary.' I didn't even know that they had recorded it. I didn't even know that they had used my part that they put into this whole thing (laughs). I listened to it and went, 'Holy shit!' It's the same key! You put the same record on one thing and the other record on the other thing side-by-side and it's almost identical. That was my intro too, those first few chords of the song. But I can't remember anything else that I was involved with."

"Too Much of Nothing" is nearly proto-doom like Sabbath, buttressed by low, low bass tones and a slow motion drum beat that stands out front just like Bill Ward's on *Black Sabbath*'s seminal title track. Phil had run out of lyrics, so it was up to Pete to come up with the words for this one. "Dance Your Life Away" follows, upholding the album's hard rock stance, albeit in funk mode, Phil using dance and dance marathon imagery to make a point about burning the candle at both ends. "This Kid's Including Between the Walls" closes, and at six minutes it is the album's epic, sent more so that way through its stuttering, circular riff, its halting drums, its multiple parts, all of them heavy until the positively elegiac "Between the Walls" segment, a near funereal outro that again recalls Black Sabbath's wake-bound material. Phil's lyric manages a palpable sense of urgency, again Mogg well within his rights as a documenter of street life and the need for the young and impressionable to escape in the face of probable death from temptation.

In February 1975, once the band and Leo had finished putting the record together, Michael promptly collapsed with a liver infection and was whisked off to the hospital where he spent six weeks, followed by a couple more months of rest at home in London. Remarked Michael to Pop magazine in Germany, "It really looks as if someone there above has got something against us. I cannot stand it at the hospital anymore as there were only loud old people there talking dog races all the time. The other three UFOs, Phil, Andy and Pete, have proved as genuine friends these days. They have come to see me almost every day, and not for a second considered to abandon me to pursue their own career. Perhaps all this bad luck is a sign of something good coming soon."

Once recovered, the band mounted a small European tour, playing France, Germany and Switzerland, highlight being a festival gig in Düsseldorf in front of a crowd of 8,000. However, scotching a gig in France due to voltage issues, the band had their tour bus pelted by rocks and bottles by the rioting crowd. Then they had some of their cables and wires stolen, their car caught fire, and Phil was whacked in the head by Pete's bass, requiring stitches. This would be a recurring theme over the years with Pete, whether it be collisions on stage with his headstock or with Way himself.

Up into 2007, *Force It* saw CD reissue, Chrysalis adding five live tracks but also "A Million Miles," a worthy finished original, essentially a power ballad with mellow verses and a stomping chorus over which Phil belts out his vocal at the top end of his range and power.

Said Melody Maker of *Force It*, "Okay, man, so you're into rock which fancies itself as art; try Yes or Wakeman. You like a bit of crudity with your rock 'n' roll; give the Feelgoods a spin. How about volume—the kind that beats you to your knees—and a riff which kicks you in the head while you're down, a lead guitar line which slices you upwards from the stomach—that's *Force It*, or at least the dominant part of the album. In between the volume and the brashness, there are a couple of moments which serve as breathing spaces before the next aural assault. Despite the basic riff formation of most of the songs on *Force It*, UFO sound a cut above most of the bands currently doing the rounds with this brash style. Leo Lyons has brought out all of the strong points in the band, and if there are any weaknesses, he's hidden them well. UFO have been flying since 1971—it's about time they were sighted by a few more people."

Record Mirror was also complimentary, making comparisons to Wishbone Ash, and even "the dean of rock critics," Robert Christgau, no fan of anything heavy, thought the album a palatable and smart form within a distasteful genre of rock.

Not that Phil put much faith in what the critics were saying, telling Scene magazine, "One week a reviewer really slams the record, attacking the band personally more than our music, but the next week we get a great review in the same paper from another bloke on the same album. It's like they're very conscious of American responses to acts, and they saw *Force It* moving strongly into the US charts."

"It might be confidence in Jim Beam," adds Phil, talking about the band's attendant live success, "but really, we have to feel that way. We've gone into places without any publicity machine behind us, done our show, and drawn twice as many the next time with no one but ourselves having done it. The last album even surprised the record company with how well it did. One executive told me he'd ask people about UFO and they had never heard of us, and he would quote them our sales figures and they wouldn't believe it. We can't help but be confident, because we've more or less done what we've done ourselves; no one's given us any of it."

UK rock critic royalty was also paying attention to the proto-heavy metal charms of UFO even at this early stage, none other that Geoff Barton writing in Sounds, "Already an American chart-breaker and packaged in a clever double entendre Hipgnosis cover, *Force It* is a raucous, pounding album, the sort that will shake those delicate china ornaments on your mantelpiece apart and then progressively reduce them to fine dust. UFO are a pleasantly competent heavyweight band—the compositions are concise but varied, full of interchanging riffs, Phil Mogg is a nasty vocalist and Michael Schenker can play guitar as scalding as the hot tap, or as icy as the cold one." The master influencer helps put UFO on the map onward and upward by pronouncing *Force It*, "a worthy successor to *Phenomenon*." As the years roll on, Barton would be there at every step, helping shape opinion, mostly favourably, on this fine British institution of a band.

Chapter Six
No Heavy Petting

"On the one hand there's a tree,
and on the other hand there's what you do"

History has proven that *Force It* is a classic UFO album, if only for the fact that it coughed up a trio of UFO anthems in "Let It Roll," "Shoot Shoot" and "Mother Mary." Detractors could asterisk that with the grouse that the versions therein enclosed are not exactly stellar, played and recorded spare and boxy, and that the album as a whole still had a leaden, sodden, rudimentary quality. Not so with *No Heavy Petting*. If one could argue that *Phenomenon* was the first modern and professional UFO album, and then the same all over again for *Force It* with its up-quotient of riff rock, one could also delay those accolades until *No Heavy Petting*, which most definitely kicked the band up another notch in sophistication of arrangement, in tone, in production values, in such abstracts as confidence, bravado and intelligence.

"Personally I like *No Heavy Petting* better because it was more mature," says Michael, knocking the nail on the head. "*Force It* was a rocking album. *No Heavy Petting* was a bit more polished. I couldn't believe it. *No Heavy Petting* didn't do that good sales-wise, and I was kind of confused about it. But I think they had a problem at the record company at the time and that could have been the reason. But I personally like that one better than *Force It*. But I was happy actually with all the albums, *Phenomenon*, *Force It*, and yes, *No Heavy Petting* especially. You grow and as life changes, you have different attitudes and obviously everything else changes with it. You have five people in the band, and everybody changes in their own ways and puts in their input. It's like that with everything. You change clothing, different generations; things look and act differently."

Continues Schenker, "*No Heavy Petting* could have been a really, really good album—with Ron Nevison. But everybody noticed by that time that a producer was needed, and I also wanted an additional musician in the band who would be able to give me like a screen to paint on, like a keyboard player/guitarist, something I could play to, rather than just to bass, with limited notes and space. Anyway, when Paul Raymond and Ron Nevison came in, it was a complete picture."

So it was more or less Michael's idea to get a keyboardist. "I don't know if it was my idea. But I wasn't happy playing to nothing. I wanted something with more than the four strings of the bass. I wanted something to make me more inspirational. Because when you play the break and you only have a bass, it just comes across differently than if you have more notes behind it. Because then it indicates whether it is a minor or major, which will then help people understand what you're trying to do. If you don't have that, it's more difficult for the consumer to understand what you're trying to do."

Added Pete on getting keys into the mix, speaking with Marko Syrjala, "At the time it was lot of work for Michael as a four-piece. Some of the songs had a lot of overdubs and keyboards were on the albums. So it was like, let's try keyboards. We found that just having keyboards on their own was too much. We didn't have them on all the time; it would be just for intros and some sophisticated parts. That's how Paul Raymond became involved, because Paul plays a good rhythm guitar and of course is a really good keyboard player, so that fitted. Michael and I couldn't reproduce the backing of the albums as close as we would've liked to. Some people really liked it as a four-piece, but sometimes you've got songs like for instance 'Love to Love,' things that do have those keyboard pieces. In those days you couldn't use samples; they didn't appear from nowhere. We've always been a very realistic live band."

"Gung ho. Excuse me, could you please get out of our way?" is the way Phil describes the band vibe at the time of both *No Heavy Petting* and *Force It*, two records that are often looked on as a pair, in the organizing minds of fans. "We were gung ho; they're fresh and crisp and I really like those. There are some really good tunes on there."

"We treated everything the same," offers Pete. "We still do today.

We don't let prima donnas in the band. When Michael is great, Michael's great. When Danny is great, Danny's great. We go in to enjoy ourselves, record, and make a great rock record. It's like a gang thing we did. We could still be in the school playground today, when I work with the boys. Danny is a rock star. I like Danny a lot. Good. Danny added a certain thing, some great stuff to us. Difficult to say, really. Well... good! If you was to ask me, when people get a bit tired after three years of working together, or being on the road in America, which we did for a long time, sort of hours being together and getting fed up with one another's company, you can say yeah, once in awhile arguments happened. But I haven't got any bad memories particularly of anybody I've worked with. The funny thing is, I've never listen to keyboards unless they're absolutely necessary. But for me, UFO is a three-piece rock band with a singer."

The Danny of which Pete speaks is one Danny Peyronel, an Argentinean by birth, brought in on keyboards and sent out by the next album, even though his role was crucial in taking the band to the next musically professional level.

Danny tells the story of leaving The Heavy Metal Kids to become one of the boys. "I had a friend called Paul Varley who was in my first-ever professional band, just before The Kids, The Rats. Paul was the drummer, lovely guy. He knew both The Kids and UFO, and he was a great mate of Pete's. We had been to America with The Kids and... really strange, you know, one of those moments when you're in the Holiday Inn with nothing to do, waiting to be picked up. I switched on the telly, and it was Don Kirshner's Rock Concert, and the boys were on, UFO. I went, 'I remember; Paul is a friend of theirs.' When I finished the tour and went back, Paul calls me up and introduces me to Pete and Pete asks me to a gig, and he comes to our gig and so on and so forth."

The lynchpin event came from the band having keyboards at the ready for a song off of *Force It* that they couldn't play live without keyboards. Peyronel was asked to sit it, in Cologne, Germany, and his first memory of his entrance into the band was of Michael waiting on the steps of the hotel to greet him. That night was a free night, so the boys got down to some partying, while the next day they routined "Out in the Street," which they played together that night, with Danny also joining them for the "C'mon Everybody" encore. August 22nd 1975, Peyronel was officially on as a member of the band, playing the

Friday at the Reading Festival.

Danny seems somewhat aghast that Michael was a bit of a catalyst and plumper for the idea of a keyboardist in the band. "Really? (laughs). That's the first time I've heard that! That's quite far-fetched, because when the time came that I got the boot, I understood that he kind of thought that he would prefer another guitarist or something, or keyboard player that can play guitar. Or rather, somebody rather than a keyboard player. I understood that that was the case. But you never know when that happens. You never know what the truth is. But I got along with him really great on the road. I put him to bed many a' time that he was lying in the hallway (laughs)."

Peyronel indicates at that point that drugs weren't impeding the band. "No, no, no, just alcohol. Alcohol was huge, especially with him, of course. But I thought he was a good kid. Because he spoke very bad English in those days, I guess he kind of drifted to me because I wasn't English either. So he had something in common with me, although obviously I speak English fucking perfectly (laughs). But he just drifted to me and I thought he was a very nice kid. He just had a big problem, the drinking thing. He was very introverted and of course very insecure. He felt really alone on the road, so much that we were kind of pressured to fly his girlfriend over. Because otherwise it would've been a disaster. Well, it was a disaster (laughs), so we flew his girlfriend over. And then he calmed down completely. That was one of the tours, anyway."

Danny goes a bit more into the chemistry—or lack thereof—between Michael and the rest of the band, on a personal level. "I don't think it was a persecution. You see, you've got to understand that these other guys, right, Phil and Pete and Andy, had been together since school kind of thing. So they were like neighbourhood mates. It was very different. So they have their own little sense of humour—not too funny either (laughs). Especially when you came from the Heavy Metal Kids, which is more of a Monty Python-type thing. These guys are more like schoolboy humour, which can also be cool, but it's a different thing."

"So they had these little jokes, these little ongoing routines, about Andy, which, it was difficult to relate to for anybody coming from the outside, let alone someone like Michael, who's German as well. He's got that going against him (laughs). But it's not the same sense of humour. I don't know if they ribbed him at all. I mean, they ribbed me a helluva lot too, but I just ignored it. Understood what the game was; not a problem. So it wasn't particularly Michael. I remember how meticulous he was. Remember how he did all those loads of harmony parts to these lead parts that he did, right? That was very German; I thought that was very well done. He would do each part separately. Of course, he would have to get the vibrato exactly in the same places for it to sound like one massive guitar. It was very meticulous, very interesting, that. It's amazing how professional he could be."

In that sense, there are two guitarists in particular, Brian May and Michael Schenker, that can be inserted on their lonesome into the family tree of twin lead innovators, which runs roughly from the Allman Brothers, Wishbone Ash, Thin Lizzy and Judas Priest through to Iron Maiden, who of course are huge UFO devotees.

"Oh, he's very serious, yes," agrees Leo Lyons on Schenker, Lyons back as the band's producer for a third record. "Unbelievably serious, you know. You can work it out. If you've got a budget of £1,000, or £2,000, say £150 a day, and the guy does a great guitar solo and you say, 'That was fantastic, Michael' and then he'd say, 'Well, for you maybe.' He'd need to do another 15 and then you'd take bars and bits out of each, and I think that followed on pretty much all the way through his career. But then he's a perfectionist."

Lyons adds that Michael would work out everything ahead of time and get to a final usable version through repetition and precision, often after the boys had long given up and gone to the pub. But the implication of the above is that you could burn through those notoriously meagre UFO budgets pretty quickly, budgets that grew by leaps and bounds for the next record, in part, apparently, because Chrysalis eventually felt or realised that they had dropped the ball on the band by under-funding them.

"We were on such a tight budget," elaborates Leo. "The record company, I think they gave me £1,000 for *Phenomenon*, and if you think it's £200 a day, I maybe managed to squeeze six days out of them. The next one, I think they gave me a couple thousand pounds and the next one they gave me maybe a couple thousand pounds, maybe £3,000 to do it. So they were all incredibly tight. I mean, we couldn't spend three or five days getting a drum track. You had to be realistic, do maybe three backing tracks a day. I'm sure we did some stuff, including basic stuff like putting the guitar through a Leslie, delays and things like that. But really, there's no time to experiment when you're that tight. When things are that tight, you've got to go for it." So no string arrangements. "No, golly, we couldn't have afforded strings! £1,500 including the strings, folks. You have ten days (laughs)."

It is of note that Leo has also been cited in interviews as recalling that the recording sessions lasted about ten, fifteen and twenty days respectively, for each successive album, albeit he might have been including mixing in those numbers.

"The first record we did, nobody in the record company believed in the band," says Leo, comparing all three he did with UFO. "In fact, it took three records to get the record company to believe in the band (laughs). I mean, I was excited by all three. I always think that the first record is... I know UFO had some records out before, but we take it as one of the first records in their commercial career. They've got all the material, they're playing it live on stage and you go in and do that pretty quickly. The second record, you're trying quite hard but I think we managed to come up with some material. The third record, it becomes difficult. So the first record was, I think, probably more spontaneous and the following two, we were really having to work hard on them."

Leo recalls the hard graft of having to work at Morgan, in Willesden (after an initial set of sessions at Wessex), while living on a farm in Oxfordshire, and the long commutes home in the middle of the night, barely fending off sleep. Eventually he hired a driver.

"My favourites... I mean, 'Rock Bottom' and 'Doctor Doctor' are UFO career songs, I think," continues Lyons. "But we had 'Shoot Shoot' on *Force It*, which was actually a hit single for them in some countries. I like them all. My production philosophy really is to try to get the best out of the band, see what potential I think they have and help them realise it. I don't try and go in with a definite idea of how it's going to sound, unless it's something I'm doing myself. In other words, if I've written a song and I'm playing on it, everything on it, then maybe I do have an idea. I think if you start thinking about, 'What did I do most on?' then you're not doing your job. You just make it happen. I think the guys were pretty disciplined, compared with the persona that you see, you know, 'Here they are, they're all drunk again and they're all on drugs and they're going crazy.' They were pretty disciplined in the studio. I mean, I don't know how they were working with other people. But certainly, when I worked with them, you know, I had put together a team of people and we worked as a team, and hopefully before I actually commit to working with someone on a project, we all have a pretty common direction."

"Nobody ever told me that," laughs Danny when asked why he thought UFO did in fact end up with a keyboard player: "But what I'm guessing at is that since that last album, *Force It*, had keyboards on it—Chick Churchill had played—I'm guessing that it was, 'Well, it sounds nice with a bit of keyboards.' How it all came about was that I was in Germany, and it all really came to a head with The Kids, because of the guitarist we had and we didn't get along. So I said, 'Look, I'm going to go. Rather that, than the band splits up. You go ahead.' Because half was with me and half was with the guitarist (laughs). So the boys were in Germany on tour as well, so I phoned my girlfriend—who is still with me, by the way—and she got in touch with the Chrysalis office, and they told me where they were. So The Kids dropped me off where they were. Pete said, 'Oh, fucking great, you're here. Because, we've brought a piano in the truck, and we've got all these songs we can't do, you know, from the album. It would be great if you did a couple of them.' 'Yeah, sure.' But no, I don't know if it was fortuitous or they were having this idea already because of the album."

"It took about a month, I believe," recalls Danny, on the assembly of *No Heavy Petting*. "Which was a luxury for me, because the first two Heavy Metal Kids records took seven and nine days. Morgan Studios was a bit dilapidated already, up in Willesden, I think, North London. I remember the boys from Judas Priest were next door and they were huge fans of Schenker of course. But then, they weren't really famous. Later Morgan Studios had become The Power Plant. A friend of mine—I had played guitar in a band we had together—bought it and produced from there. He became the producer of Sade, made millions, and he's a brilliant guitarist too, a guy named Robin Miller; he bought the studio and it's now called The Power Plant. But Leo, he's a lovely, lovely guy. As a producer, which is a matter of opinion, I thought he was all right. But as a guy, he's just a wonderful person. He was just a really good solid producer."

"I don't remember; we didn't hang out," answers Danny, asked if Priest were recording *Sad Wings of Destiny*. "We talked a bit when we bumped into them but at that time, we kind of used to make fun of the singer (laughs). Because he didn't look like he looks now, or like he looked later. He used to dress like a dandy, right? Very foolish (laughs). With a silver-topped cane and a cape. I'm sorry, but you can imagine Pete, right? It couldn't be helped. And they became huge, right? With all the leather and stuff later, he looked totally menacing. But no big parties or anything recording. It was all very English (laughs). Which is completely different from America. It was just, 'Pardon?' We were just working. As usual in England, we were doing it in January or February which is just fucking freezing (laughs). But perhaps that accounts for many good records. The fact that you have that horrible weather makes you want to be inside making good music. We'd work from early afternoon all the way until late, whenever, three in the morning. Long hours."

Asked about Judas Priest, Andy says that, "Phil was telling me he saw Glenn Tipton fairly recently and he looked great. They were another band that I always thought had a reputation that I never really saw. I thought they were just straight guys that we've known for so long. They probably felt we had a reputation for being crazy too."

"I believe we were, but that's a difficult thing to answer to," remarks Parker, on the subject of who would have headlined shows between UFO and Judas Priest in the '70s, when they crossed paths, which turned out to be quite often. "Because there were situations with AC/DC for example, where we did loads of shows with AC/DC in the '70s, and depending on what part of the market we were in, we would switch. In some areas UFO was stronger and in some areas AC/DC was stronger, and depending where you were, you switched the headliner. There's a good chance that happened with Judas Priest as well. In the early days probably we were, but then obviously they became a huge act. So I'm sure we opened for them. With Glenn, we knew him from even before Judas Priest. He had a band called The Flying Hat Band, and we were with the same agency, way back, in the early '70s."

"Let me tell you a story; have you met Glenn? He just loves a good story. He was telling us—and it was probably with the Hat Band and not with Priest, but I wouldn't swear to it. They were up north somewhere and they had bought some English fast food, which is a bit scary. They had this pie that they had bought. He was sitting in the van eating this pie, and it was absolutely foul, it was awful, he couldn't eat it. So they said, 'Oh, wind the window down,' and they dropped the window, and they launched this pie out of the window.

Unfortunately they were driving past a bus stop at the town. There was this guy at the bus stop and this thing, it hit him in the neck. Obviously it was really hot and it awfully hurt this guy, and apparently this guy chased the van for... Glenn said he just thought this guy was never going to stop. They would pull up to a traffic light and the guy started gaining on them (laughs). He would be banging on the side of the van. He was saying, 'This guy, you could see him in the side mirror.' Glenn thought he was going to kill somebody. He was just chasing this van for fucking miles, and they were just trying to get away from him. 'Quick, go! He's gaining on us!' God knows who he was, but you can imagine pulling up at a light, 'He's gaining on us!' Glenn's a funny guy."

"But yeah, we had a lot of good times spent together," continues Andy. "Funny enough, years ago, the early days of UFO, and UFO were doing really well, Glenn was struggling to find a drummer, and actually we were having a conversation. I thought about leaving UFO and I remember him saying, 'You know, if you ever thought about coming in, it'd be great; I'd cut you in the band.' But obviously, like I said, UFO were doing real well then so it didn't cross my mind. But it's interesting how different it would have been had I decided to do that. It's just interesting how fortunes change and things move. I mean, we used to all go off and be in the same hotel with them. Always good for a laugh Mr. Tipton. They were a great band and a great bunch of guys and I'm glad to still see them doing well. And I remember, actually after UFO broke up in '83, I was in a plane flying from California to London and Glenn was on the plane and I remember him saying, 'It's really sad that you guys are gone. There's only really you and us left, from these kind of bands.' And I said, 'Yeah, I know—things happen.' We were in sort of self-destruct mode then but who knew we'd rise from the ashes again?"

In pre-release press materials put together by Warner Bros., who was distributing Chrysalis product in the US, Phil Mogg warned of an "absolute full frontal attack this time." Mogg also deems "Martian Landscape" "a mystical piece which builds to a tremendous crescendo at the end," while also promising that the new five-man line-up "can now use our dynamics a lot more in concert. We can recreate our records more faithfully. All our resources as a group are pooled instantaneously on stage. We look very sexual on stage and me move better than anyone else."

Writer of the piece Joe Robinson said that, "I'm a Loser"

Left: The original UFO; left to right: Phil Mogg, Pete Way, Andy Parker and Mick Bolton.

Right: A rare shot of a band briefly in flux. Clockwise from top: Andy Parker, Phil Mogg, Pete Way and Andy Parker.

Below: Assorted ancient evidence of a band that was active and making somewhat of a worldwide impact.

On tour in America in support of *No Heavy Petting*. The common denominator? Keyboardist Danny Peyronel in every shot! (courtesy of Nigel Hart)

Publicity shot from 1975. Left to right: Michael Schenker, Andy Parker, Pete Way, Danny Peyronel and Phil Mogg. (courtesy of Nigel Hart)

Below: Clockwise from left: Chrysalis was generally pretty good with placing ads in the English entertainment weeklies, as well as maintaining some of the creative spirit injected into the album cover art by Hipgnosis; Obscure release for "Rock Bottom;" Danny's back!

Phil Mogg takes a break and then rallies, Tulsa, Oklahoma, 1977. (*courtesy of Rich Galbraith*)

Top: A propped-up Pete Way (*courtesy of Rich Galbraith*)
Bottom: UFO in guitar army mode. Left to right: Paul Raymond, Michael Schenker and Pete Way, with Phil peeking out from behind the marauding bassist.
(*courtesy of Rich Galbraith*)

NEW FROM CHRYSALIS

A SURGE OF POWER FROM

UFO

WITH THEIR NEW ALBUM

LIGHTS OUT

CHR 1127

PRODUCED BY RON NEVISON FOR GADGET PRODUCTIONS INC.

RELEASE DATE MAY 12

AVAILABLE THROUGH EMI

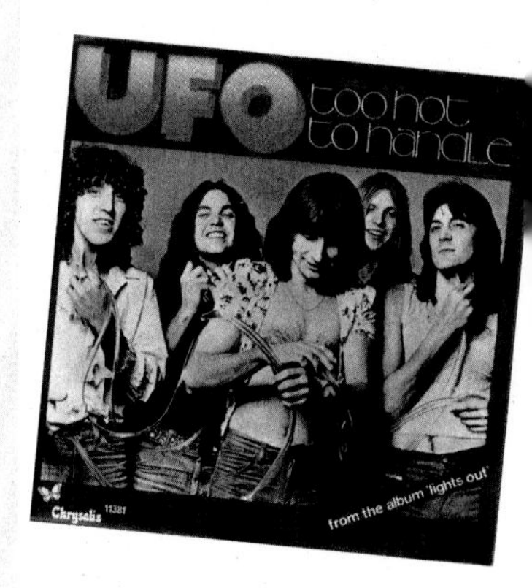

Below: UFO's most sensible member Andy Parker, althoug the gong and the two bass drums is a bit rich.
(courtesy of Rich Galbraith)

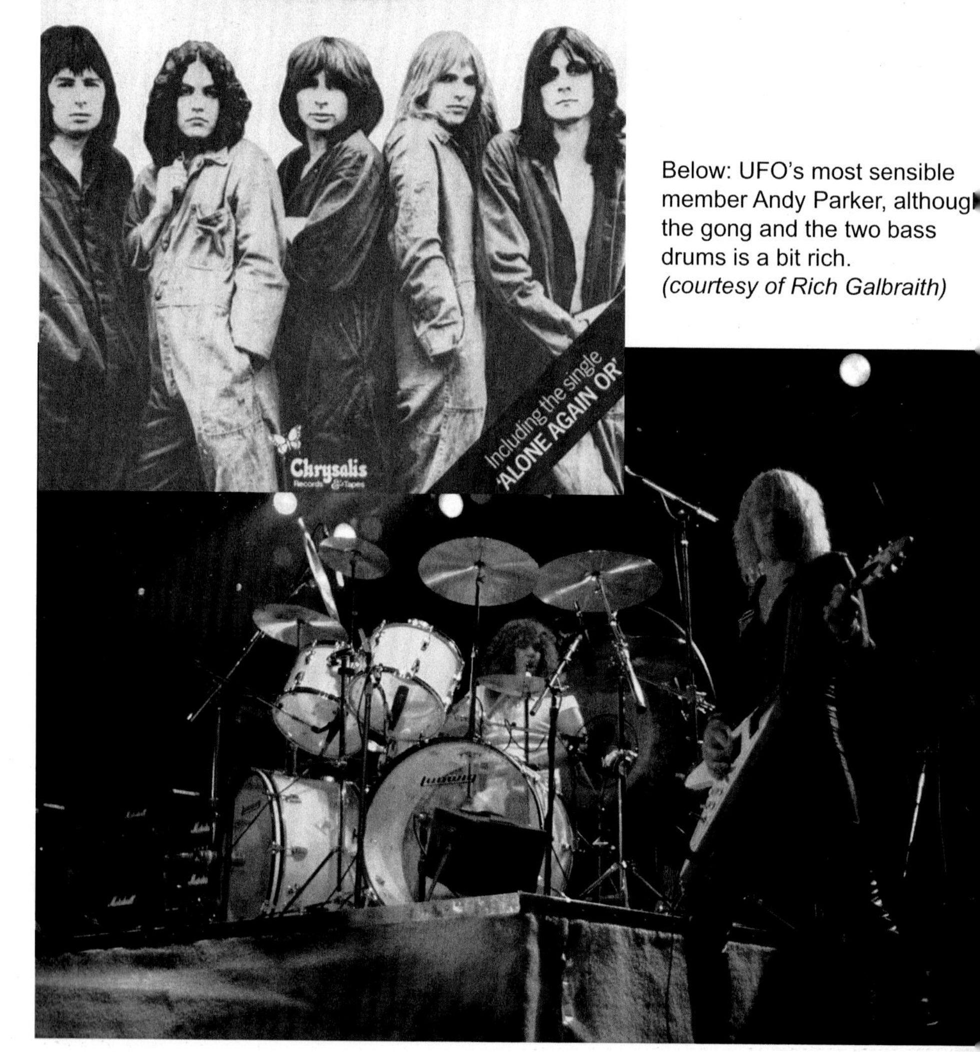

Left and below: Pete and Michael locking in, on tour in America supporting *Lights Out*, framed by two ads that both plump for the band's "heavy" credentials. *(courtesy of Rich Galbraith)*

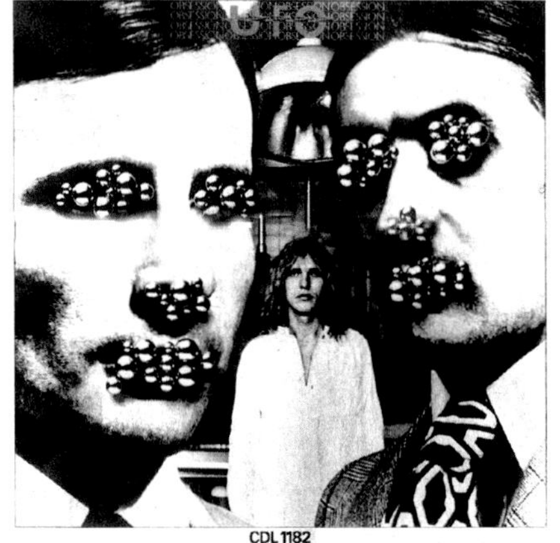

CDL 1182

OBSESSION. UFO. NEW ALBUM. HEAVY.

LONDON HAMMERSMITH ODEON. JUNE 28. LIVERPOOL EMPIRE. JUNE 29 EDINBURGH ODEON. JUNE 30. GLASGOW APOLLO. JULY 1. LEEDS GRAND THEATRE. JULY 2. IPSWICH GAUMONT. JULY 3.

.INESCAPABLE.

Wrinkly but still rocking.
Above left: Michael at The Rockpile in Toronto, 2012; above right: Phil at The Rockpile, Toronto, 2013; below: Andy at the Rockpile, 2013
(courtesy of Bill Baran)

"demonstrates a distinctive facet of UFO composing: the song veers from flat-out ear-shredding to its more melodic segments without ever breaking stride. It's a chance to check out the group's fine harmonies in the quieter moments before being hurled back into the tempest. German-born guitarist Michael Schenker is in large part responsible for this mode of writing. Like a construction worker who's a closet ballet dancer, Schenker often lets his leonine ferocity give way to the lyrical call of a solitary nightingale; witness "Belladonna." His power spot in "On with the Action" backs up his reputation as one of rock's fastest-rising guitar stars."

For an album cover, the band went with a substantially typical Hipgnosis sleeve, medical like the last one, cold and austere like so many Hipgnosis worlds created. A woman is shown participating in a blood transfusion with a monkey, creating an oblique pun in conjunction with the title. The presentation is one that could have been used for any Hipgnosis-friendly band, and indeed, the graphics house was known to shop rejected art ideas to the next band and the next band until they got the thumbs up. UFO were not moving at a speed slow enough to give a damn, and one suspects they were an easy sell with whatever was put in front of them.

No Heavy Petting, released May, 1976, kicked off with a boulder of a riff from Michael, opening wide what would be the band's "Smoke on the Water," "Natural Thing" pounding away, modulating, eventually finding a joyous boogie woogie chorus and a nice glam bit before falling back into its heavy metal pocket. In this respect, it foreshadowed the rock 'n' roll elements of later hits like "Only You Can Rock Me" and "Too Hot to Handle."

"I've never understood the attraction of 'Natural Thing'," opines Danny. "It was just a chord sequence that Schenker had, nothing more, and Phil managed to somehow (laughs), insert a melody in there, immense credit to him. Because I thought it was just a chord progression. I can't write like that. When I write the music I have to create the melody, all together. I can't just write chords. They don't mean anything to me. I guess maybe it's a guitar thing."

"I don't remember much of an input from Pete in those days," adds Danny, on the subject of Pete Way's co-credit on "Natural Thing," his only one on the album. "Because we didn't write together. I wrote with Schenker and I wrote with Andy and I wrote with Phil, but not at the same time. Phil would just take the music and do a melody and words on it. It's a shame; I probably would have enjoyed writing with Pete."

"Pete is a great songwriter," adds Michael, laughing, "very different; he's more like maybe the Rolling Stones meets The Beatles." On top of the self-evident trundle of "Natural Thing," Phil turns in a few nice turns of phrase, although the overall concept of rock 'n' rollers and the ladies they attract (and repel) is a bit weak.

The aforementioned "I'm a Loser" follows, and with its inviting, folksy acoustic passages, buttressed elegantly by piano, along with its crescendos and plot twists, it's no surprise it's a UFO classic, still a regular song in the set decades later and actually a high point at that. According to Paul Raymond (not yet in the band at this juncture), Danny should have been included in the writing credit on that one, Paul adding that it's a personal favourite. "Yes, it's one obviously I had nothing to do with but I just love the way it builds; it's got a great chord sequence and I think it's just Michael at his heyday."

Comments Danny: "In all these years, I've completely forgotten but that is true that I did some of the melodies and other musical parts. But I didn't really struggle to get it credited. I was a good part of that one but I really don't care. That was a nice song, interesting, and great words. Phil is good with words. He worked really hard on them. I don't know if it was hard or easy, but it wasn't a last-minute thing. He was very punctilious about that, very serious. That was good."

"He's very film noire," says Danny, when asked to characterise Phil as a lyricist, the "I'm a Loser" lyric capturing poetically the drift of a young punk, chip on the shoulder, and as a result, no home. "Which of course now I find really cool. It's very interesting, very verismo. Are you familiar with that term? It's a type of opera, very realistic, like Carmen realisticana, which is all about Sicily, killing and fucking vendetta (laughs). Phil's very much in that line—brute reality, film noire-type thing. Very black and white movies. That's just a feeling that I got. I don't know; it's very nice stuff; interesting, different, not your usual lyrics. I like it."

As Phil is wont to do, there's a specific place name used in the song—earlier in the album, "Natural Thing" had both Memphis and Atlanta—namely Euston Station, which is a Central London tube stop where the homeless, the drifting and the drug-addicted would tend to gather. The last train for the night has gone, it's cold as ice, but the narrator and "Ginger" don't really care. As Phil has been able to achieve time and time again, it's bleak but there's a sense of the romantic.

"I did 'Can You Roll Her' with Andy, funnily enough," says Danny on the album's barnstorming third track. "If you remember that, it really is drums-oriented. It was just fucking around with a feel, type thing. We did that together. Then of course Phil would do the lyrics." Interestingly the song is almost an early form of speed metal, but with Peyronel's pervasive keyboard line, it becomes a gorgeous example of what was to be the band's guitar/keyboard alloy. As well, Phil is roaring as a vocalist (the lyric roars as well—the sexual overtones a red herring, given the fact that the song is about outrunning the coppers on your motorbike), while Michael turns the track ever so slightly Teutonic, even though he is not present in the credits.

As Danny alludes to, the song was generated by a jam between Danny, on Hammond organ, and Andy, trying to be productive while the rest of the lads were late turning up to rehearsal. Not surprisingly, the song embodies a Deep Purple vibe, also evident in the dramatic classical chord changes that one could see Ritchie Blackmore executing.

"Oh, I loved Purple," says Andy. "I had all their early albums. They were one of the bands you looked up to. I mean Purple, Zeppelin, ELP, Sabbath, you know, were huge around that time. There were a certain number of bands that were a kind of benchmark. They were such great musicians in those bands; I mean Ian Paice, Jon Lord, Ritchie Blackmore... God, you couldn't ask for a better line up really, could you?"

From that list, it's pretty obvious Parker gravitated to the heavy rockers. Asked about other fond touring memories from that period, Andy cites, "Kiss! I mean they were pretty fucking heavy. I remember, when we first toured America we actually played the Aragon Ballroom in Chicago and the line-up was UFO, T. Rex and Kiss. Can you believe that? We opened for T. Rex and Kiss. It was pretty amazing. Peter and Paul were putting on eye makeup then, and it used to run because they'd sweat so much. Plus Alice Cooper was pretty big. Larry Wallis was a huge Alice Cooper fan. *Welcome to My Nightmare* was one of my favourite albums and we actually opened for Alice in Germany when he did that show. That was really something to watch, with the split screen and all the video stuff, pretty amazing. Great musicians too, and the same band as Lou Reed. I loved Lou Reed; that *Rock n Roll Animal* live album is still one of my all-time favourite albums, and that's the same band Alice used when we played live with him. It was great to see that band. I never actually saw Lou Reed play with that band but I actually saw Dick Wagner, Steve Hunter, those guys, and that was a great band."

"Can You Roll Her" was issued as a picture sleeve single in Japan, backed with "Belladonna." A second seven-inch paired "Highway Lady" and "A Fool in Love." Surprisingly, there were no singles issued elsewhere, Chrysalis missing an opportunity to make the album more of a success, particularly with the irresistible charms of "Highway Lady."

The aforementioned "Belladonna" is next. A stark contrast to its predecessor, the song is a classically-tinged ballad, entirely quiet, without drums, featuring some beautiful soloing from Michael. Phil's lyric hints at a love-torn suicide but there's also a whiff of drug addiction to it, belladonna, also known as deadly nightshade, being used historically as an anaesthetic and a poison. Phil sings, "the fingers are poisoned like needles" and "the tea so delicately laced." In fact, belladonna, in small doses, has even been used throughout history as a recreational drug, and even an eye-drop to make women look more seductive.

"Reasons Love" crashes the calm, Andy punctuating Michael's cyclonic riff with a one-and-four snare beat, resulting in a track that would have fit proudly on *Virgin Killer* by Scorpions, Schenker's distorted tone and piercing solo being metal all the way, Phil's spiteful lyric appropriately thorned.

"Highway Lady" is credited solely to Danny Peyronel, and is a rousing, buoyant, power-packed yet melodic rocker in the fine road tale tradition. "'Highway Lady' is about prostitutes," laughs Danny. "I think it's fairly evident, road girls. There really isn't much to say. I wrote it specifically at that time for UFO." As with "Can You Roll Her," keyboards are pervasive, and even a little out of place and intrusive on the song. In effect, it's a guitar rocker turned distinct—and distinctly UFO—by this ploy.

Next up is "On with the Action," which is another very Scorpions-like track, very Teutonic, mournful, leaden, deliberate and surging... classic. The musical sound picture offers a dramatic milieu for some convincing street-tough storytelling from Phil, who bolsters the tale with knifings, doorway sex, a tragic gay figure, and finally a minister who distresses, bible in hand, at the continuing transgressive action, night after hell-bound night. Not only does Phil pack a lot of character portraits into one song, but he manages to weave their tales of trauma together.

"We were just jamming with Schenker; he started off with the riff and I started doing the chords," offers Peyronel. "There were three mistakes that were on the album with respect to the credits, all related to me (laughs). 'On with the Action,' which I'm not credited on at all, I co-wrote with Schenker in the dressing room of a San Francisco club we were playing. I've got a picture, in fact, of that moment (laughs), funnily enough. But yes, I've got a picture of that dressing room with Schenker jamming. That's how that started."

"A Fool in Love" is the album's second to last track, and is in fact a cover, penned by Free's Andy Fraser and notorious souse Frankie Miller, prolific Chrysalis Records artist and pioneering pub rocker. Says Danny, "Frankie was great; he's dead now. Doing that may have had something to do with the fact that he was on Chrysalis as well (laughs). What a shame. I remember going with the boys, UFO—in San Francisco, I think it was—to see Frankie at some club. We had already recorded there I think. It was like a really big break for him, doing this club. All sorts of press, record company people were down there, and he totally blew it! Totally out to lunch. Some people, they need to press the panic button, self-destruct." The track is a typically rootsy, Stones type track of Miller's, perfect for the newly swaggering UFO, honky-tonk piano by Peyronel being just what the doctor ordered.

Adds Leo, "We were looking for some material and we were a little short. I had actually been working with Frankie doing some development stuff with him, before he got signed. I'd always liked his songwriting so I played the guys some of his stuff, and that's what they picked. But I mean, I think it was because we were short of material, rather than 'Hell, let's do a cover.'"

Closing the album was "Martian Landscape," a dark and dreamy epic ballad, typical of the murky vibe of an earlier record, *Phenomenon*. "Lyrically, it was a real wishful thinking song about Argentina," reveals Peyronel. "I was born in Buenos Aires. There's no fucking way it's as lovely as that (laughs). It wasn't about Mars, it was about Argentina, in a figurative sense, I guess. That's how it came about. Schenker did a lovely job of it with the guitars." Indeed he does, adding some sinewy harmony solo lines which cross baroque music with George Harrison.

All told, *No Heavy Petting* turned out to be as hard-hitting as *Force It* but it was also brighter, bolder, more expressive. As a result, its reputation, always strong, has maintained or gotten stronger over the years.

Wrote Geoff Barton from Sounds, clearly in a prog rock mood, "This, UFO's third album to feature guitarist Michael Schenker, is undoubtedly the best so far, being brimful of concise, subtly dramatic, well executed rock songs. Note that I say, 'songs' rather than "numbers' or 'tracks' or 'cuts'—because songs they most definitely are. Each of the nine on the album is a precise, well-disciplined whole, laced with just the right amount of powerpack guitar and vocals, liberally sprinkled with reflective moments. Which is all well and good. Yet, *No Heavy Petting*, with successive plays, begins to sound too formalised, too finely honed, rounded at the edges. I'd love to see the band let rip and throw variation out the window; I'd like to have them try their hand at a genuine ballad, something like 'Belladonna' but taken a whole step further. But most of all, UFO should do their best to break away from the five-minutes-or-under format for each song and record a real epic, upwards of ten minutes long, where the aforementioned expertise at combining the subtle and the not so subtle could be used to the fullest possible extent."

When asked what songs were rolled out off the album on the ensuing tour, Danny suggests "'Highway Lady,' 'Can You Roll Her'... we used to open with 'Can You Roll Her,' I think. 'I'm a Loser,' 'Natural Thing;' that's about it. We may have tried 'On with the Action' a couple of times. Although we may have tried pretty much all of them, except for 'Belladonna.' I think the Frankie Miller song we did live. We may have really tried every song at least once and then shelved them (laughs). The boys had so much good material anyway."

Reflected Danny on his role in the band, specifically on stage, during all this, "I'm not really a keyboard player. That's really a bit of a misnomer for me. I'm mainly a piano player and a Hammond player. I'm not really a keyboard player. I don't do synthesizers and progressive things like that. Yes, I played one on the record, but it was a little thing. It wasn't a big thing. I was mainly a piano player. It was mainly honky-tonk piano; that's what I do. I'm not really that technical. I always felt part of the rhythm section, as a keyboard player. My brother is a drummer and everything. I grew up playing like that, really rhythmically. Not so much your florid stuff. We did some stuff in harmony live, which was quite exciting, some lead bits in harmony on the synth, with Schenker. On some of the *Force It* and *Phenomenon* songs, in fact."

The first leg found the band trotting around in the spring of '76 with Dirty Tricks and Nutz in tow, while US dates featured pairings with the likes of Nazareth, Foghat and Styx. An interesting addition to some of the shows found the band working their way through a rendition of Billy Preston's "You Are So Beautiful." A highlight of the US swing found the band on the bill for one of Bill Graham's Day on the Greens, 1st May 1976, along with Fleetwood Mac, Peter Frampton and Gary Wright. Billed as "The British Are Back," this was a follow-up to the previous year's "The British Are Coming" bill. Subsequent North American dates had the band opening for Rick Wakeman, Rainbow, J. Geils Band, Foghat, Dave Mason and label mates Jethro Tull, with Phil quipping that after listening to chants of "Tull! Tull! Tull!" he kept thinking, "We're not dull!"

Asked about the band's first venture to the American west coast, Michael offers the following reminiscence, and how things have changed for him over his career since way back when. "Well, I'll tell you one thing I will probably never forget. We came over to the states, and we had, I think, our first show in San Francisco, The Winterland, and there were 6,000 people before we came onstage, or while we were playing, with their lighters on. It was unbelievable (laughs). It was so incredible, I had to write to my brother and tell him what was going on here. But it was the only show. All the other shows were nothing like that. But I don't know, San Francisco, right from the beginning up to this day, have had the most incredible audiences, and in Chicago, kind of after we did the live album."

"And then the rest of the world," continues Michael, "basically now, at this point in time, the audiences have become almost equal throughout the world. Which is nice, because all the people that were there for the parties and because it was hip and all of that kind of stuff, they have been filtered out, and now it is only the hardcore fans left. And hardcore fans are hardcore fans. There are the same hardcore fans everywhere in the world. So it is much more enjoyable to play these days. I've changed a lot. I'm not as shy anymore and I'm enjoying being on stage more than I ever did. And just life in general is much more pleasant because I'm not as much of a perfectionist as I used to be. Being a perfectionist kind of puts you in a stupid place, really, if you think about it. I know it does, because it makes you feel very, very tense, and that's not a nice feeling. So I don't know what happened, but somehow I realised that, 'Michael, why do you spend so much time on being so perfect?' Nobody will ever notice. Somehow it clicked that it wasn't the perfectionism that was going to do the talking, it was simply the feel, the flow."

Even though Michael (and Pete) both remember San Francisco as the first show in California, the debut California appearances consisted of two nights at the Whisky A Go Go in LA (excepting a special Record Plant special gig), as stated in a tour diary article Michael wrote at the time, published in German magazine Pop, in July 1976.

A portion of the piece in translation reads as follows (some degree of grammar and punctuation altered for consistency sake): "We landed at the Los Angeles International Airport and were met by an enormous heat there. Almost 40 degrees in the shade! There was ten degrees on departure in London 12 hours before. Nobody gets over this change of climate without prejudice. Luckily we had the first three days off to acclimatize. We stayed on Sunset Boulevard at Hyatt House Hotel of ill repute. Most musicians stay there and there are lots of groupies hanging out. We have heard many stories about the hotel before and they all proved to be true. Sometimes it was worse than in a Chinese brothel. In any case we accustomed well."

"The first show took place at the Record Plant Studio. Yes, at the recording studio in front of the public. The whole show was aired live on the radio in Los Angeles. We played two sold-out shows in Los Angeles afterwards as headliners, so the radio advert really paid off. The next station was San Francisco. Two nights we played at Bill Graham's Winterland. These were the best organised concerts we have ever had. 6,000 fans cigarette lighters in the air—for us this was the greatest success of the whole tour."

"Canada was next. There were problems on the border as they did not want to let us in. We had to wait for two hours. In Vancouver we opened for Rick Wakeman. Wakeman's public reacted very poorly to our rock. A pity. Our Manager Magoo got completely drunk. As a result of that, somebody nicked the $2,800 from his jacket backstage."

"Back in the USA for nine concerts supporting Jethro Tull. It's tough to play for Tull fans, but it was better than expected. Particularly

Oklahoma, Kansas and Ohio. We played one of the last Faces concerts at Detroit's Cobo Hall, to 15,000 people; two shows for a very enthusiastic public. They call Detroit "The Rock City" in the USA. We were all too happy after the gig and we showed it to our manager Magoo: a few bars drying ice into his hotel room bathtub water on it and the whole suite disappeared in an impenetrable fog. We did not know at all that Magoo could swear so variedly."

"The concerts with J. Geils Band in Chicago, Washington and Boston followed. The shows were great for us with encores each night—only J. Geils Band was not amused.

In Chicago, Ritchie Blackmore, the star of the night with his Rainbow, refused to play right after us. Miami was even better—white sand, palms, suntanned girls rubbing suntan oil on our backs. Two shows with Dave Mason followed. It was crazy: the crowd went wild for us. Dave Mason was greeted with "UFO! UFO" chants. The next night he opened for us. It continued to go across, over the continent, Atlanta, Sarasota, Pittsburgh Philadelphia, New York. Very beautiful but it's also a considerable strain. We all took a deep breath after the last concert in New York. Our record company threw a farewell party with large amounts of food and alcohol."

Out on the road, Phil Mogg's famous temper erupted, but really only sparingly, on occasion. "Oh dear, I'm really going to get into trouble, but I don't care," laughs Danny, recounting a bit of background on the subject of Phil's fists. "The first guitarist in the band, Mick Bolton, who was also his brother-in-law, apparently—this is what Pete tells me, and all the others tell me, so I have to think it's true, but don't quote me as saying it's true. I'm just repeating what I was told—apparently, when he got him out of the band, he punched him out of the band. That's basically what he did, his own brother-in-law. Then he did it, I think, to Bernie Marsden. Then, of course, on the road I saw him do it to a couple of roadies, who really deserved it, because they had gotten all drunk in Sweden and made us look bad. So he was waiting for them when he got back. Because apparently he had boxed as an amateur before."

"We get very energetic because your adrenaline's very high on the road," mused Pete at the time, speaking with Scene magazine. "It's the kind of excess energy that makes bands smash places up. We can't afford that ourselves, though." Added Phil, "It's difficult when you've got a lot of energy built up and then run into a day off; it breaks the momentum."

Pete, honing in on Danny's Swedish tale, totally disagrees with his assessment of Phil's violent streak. "No! You know what? They smashed up the hotel foyer. We had to go out with the record company people and they came back from the gig, and they were actually our road crew. We used to take our road crew everywhere. We're talking about two or three people. We got back, and the police were there. The foyer had been smashed up, for whatever reason, because they hadn't gone with us. Phil went and asked them something about it and he lost his temper, period, that was it. Do you really think Phil goes around doing things like that? Of course he doesn't! All he did was... imagine getting back to the hotel and they're going, 'Are you with the band? Are you with the band?' 'Well, yeah.' 'The foyer was all smashed up.' They went to have an argument and it became an argument and his temper flew because obviously he'd been having a few drinks. It's not like he premeditatedly goes out to be violent. Of course he didn't."

But Danny reaffirms that Phil's temper was at the upper end of the scale. "Phil was a little like that. It was frightening. You could see that he was upset. It would upset him that he would get violent like that. So it was a weird thing. But like I said, he never did it with me. But I understand he eventually did it with Michael, right? Well, on one of those American tours... you see, that's the difference with my Heavy Metal Kids and Tarzen experiences—this just never happened. On both American tours, especially the second one, the UFO dressing room was not a happy place, however great the gig turned out to be."

"And believe me, most times the gig was terrific and we had good crowds, great reaction and everything else. Schenker played just fucking amazingly! Okay, so instead the feeling was almost always dark. You know, 'You could've done better.' It was very upsetting. But basically it was all directed at Michael because of his drink or whatever. One particular night, I remember, he had drunk a little too much, so instead of being in-cred-ible (laughs), he was just brilliant (laughs). I mean, anybody would be happy with fucking brilliant. So after the gig, Mogg is there looking down at the floor and he's really angry, and he's saying, 'Well, yeah, of course, some of us don't know how to hold their liquor; that's the problem with this band.' Schenker cracked and he went, 'Okay, you little Hitler, why don't you hit me?' You could tell that Phil really wanted to, but was keeping himself in check (laughs), thinking, well, we need this guy. So he didn't. He was going, 'Come on, well, hit me!' I thought, no, don't keep asking (laughs). But no, he did control himself."

But, says Danny, Phil never came to blows with Pete or with Andy. "Never. Never, because, as I said he before, those were his childhood chums. First off, I would think it's, a) impossible but b) they would never provoke him. They would just never say anything too loud, or too anything. See, I kind of remember the last American tour. There was one little episode that was a little bit out for me and I kind of had the mentality of not staying around too long after that happened. That was a very simple thing, in Chicago I remember, the Aragon Ballroom. We had played with Foghat and we were sharing the bill and we went down a storm. We did like two encores and everything, and Phil got a little bit insecure and panicked. 'C'mon Everybody' was our first encore, right? Instead of leaving it for the encore, he said 'Quick, let's do "C'mon Everybody" to finish,' meaning that will guarantee an encore. It was obvious we were going to get an encore; we were going down a storm."

"But he did that, and I mentioned in the dressing room that that was a drag that we did that, because I thought it was a clear encore, and we could have had 'C'mon Everybody' as the main encore and then got two more (laughs). It wasn't a big deal; I just made a comment. He looked at me and he says, 'Well, I'm the leader of this band, right? Whatever I say goes.' Which was totally unnecessary. It was like 'What?!' (laughs). I didn't really need that kind of thing."

Moving to the subject of Pete Way, the band's second showman, co-banana to Phil so to speak and the clear rock 'n' roller bouncing around up there, Danny says that, "Pete was pretty reliable. The only things that got out of hand with him were funny things, nothing to do with alcohol or drugs or anything. Like, he would move *soooo* much onstage, that sometimes the odd bum note would happen. Which is normal (laughs). So we said to him, 'Pete, could you just give us a little bit less movement? So we don't get these bum notes in?' So he goes, 'Oh, right, you want me to stand there like a tree or something, with roots!' And we're going, 'No, on the one hand there's a tree, and on the other hand there's what you do. In the middle there's like five million gradations of what you can do' (laughs). No, he never was unreliable in those days. But we were always colliding (laughs). He would come to my mic, to sing harmonies. Well, to sing harmonies is an expression (laughs). But he would just come up there, 'C'mon everybody!' Those were the main collisions we had. I used to enjoy the live show."

Drugs were not really an issue yet, Danny indicating that with Phil, it was "just drinking and not all that much either. Just normal Englishman's drinking," adding that "Andy of course was completely level-headed and pretty much so was Pete. It's just that he wasn't a leader. So yes, Phil was in charge. We never had any big problems. The only problem was Michael. We missed the odd show, a big stadium show, because of Michael. But even with him, it wasn't horrific. I was lucky; I was in the non-horrific part (laughs)."

Asked whether with Phil and his dark mood backstage, it more critical and constructive or simply irrational, Danny figures, "Maybe a bit of both. Please be clear about this when you write it. I don't have any... I'm not criticizing him at all. I don't have any ill feeling at all towards him or any of the other boys. I do think however that he probably had some kind of problem with his dark side. Everybody has a dark side, right? His was particularly dark (laughs). We haven't spoken in ages. I've spoken with Pete and we've met each other, but the things I've heard from Phil regarding me have always been nice. I really don't have any problem with him. In fact, I'd love to see him. He looks fucking great. Even the new guys don't look as good."

I asked Peyronel to what extent Phil was involved in the business end of things. "I don't know if he was. He seemed to be very, very close with that person, Wilf Wright, who was our so-called manager. I say so-called manager, because he worked for Chrysalis *and* he was managing the band. Now, you explain to me how it is possible that an employee of the record company can be the manager of the band. Talk about conflict of interest. He was an even darker person, really introverted. Now with Phil, they seemed like big mates. So I think Phil kept everything very, very close to his chest, as did this guy. He would never say anything, or Andy. Neither did I; I was too new, really, to say anything about the business. I didn't get involved at all. I just know that I never got paid for that record, of course. Nothing. Just nothing at all. The only reason why I made money out of it is because that Wilf made a mistake, not made a mistake, but just didn't care. When it came time to... because in him not caring, I made money out of the record (laughs)."

How so? "Well, very simple. When we went to do that Swedish tour

I told you about, he flew out, and the record was coming out, and he had to do the credits thing. So he said, 'Oh, by the way, Danny, your publishing... I spoke to Atlantic's publishing,' who said they had my publishing or something. Yes, they had my publishing on the Kids records. But I had gotten a release from them, you see? He said, 'I spoke to Atlantic and they told me that as far as they're concerned, you're still with Atlantic publishing.' It was called Cotillion Music or whatever. 'So what I did is I just put your songs, Copyright Control.' Which means, when it's sorted out who owns the songs, they collect. Whether it's the band, or you can do a deal."

"So of course I had told him I was no longer with them. He just spoke with some person who didn't know what they were talking about, who said, 'Oh, no, he's still with us.' So he said, 'Oh, I can't be bothered. Copyright Control.' What that meant was that eventually I just formed my own company, which is nothing. You just say you're a company and then you can collect (laughs). I joined MCPS, which is the Mechanical Copyright Protection Society, and they collected for me ever since. Which is without any percentage paid to the publishing company, of course. So I probably made more from that record than any of the boys, because they had huge debts with Chrysalis Publishing. They wanted to put me on Chrysalis Publishing, but they didn't, because he thought, 'Oh, there's conflict here, don't want to get involved.' So they lost all that, and I got it, which was good."

Peyronel's tenure with the band was short-lived, although he did manage to get in a couple of tours of America.

"Yes, one would have been '75, around when the Reading Festival is on, September or something, end of August. The other one was shortly after that. We came back, I remember, because it was very funny. We did a whole lot of gigs, right? Started out in LA, did the midwest and everything. We did a whole bunch of gigs with Peter Frampton, including Washington DC, I think. On that first one we did Canada as well, but not Toronto. We did Montreal and all that, with Rick Wakeman, which was weird (laughs). But we did these shows with Frampton and he was really dying and we were going down better than him. He was above us, and then J. Geils was the top of the bill. So I remember overhearing his manager saying, 'If you don't do it soon, I'm dropping you!' It was really sad. So we go home, right? (laughs). This is how things used to happen then. We go home to England for like a week, maybe ten days and we go back, right? When we go back, in those ten days or two weeks tops, the first gig we have, Oakland Stadium, Peter Frampton, top of the bill, because in the meantime, that live record had come out. So suddenly he's massive. How weird is this? That doesn't happen now."

The European tours, explains Danny, were, "on our own. Especially in Germany; we were big in Germany already then. We did a tour of festivals just before we went to America for the first time. I mean, that shows you how well regarded the band was in Europe, especially in Germany. It was a last-minute thing. They got us a special guest, without advertising, in like five or six festivals. Special guest billing and everything. Which denotes that they had some pull there. We just did Germany and Scandinavia."

As a side note, Danny in fact had joined UFO in August '75, a mere three months after the release of *Force It*, as mentioned, jumping right into the fire by debuting at the Reading Festival. Danny can be heard playing live in the studio with the band on September 23rd '75 at The Record Plant in Los Angeles, a performance captured on assorted bootlegs as well as the *Big Apple Encounters* CD, released by Majestic in 2003. The name of this semi-official (or at least most-known) version, along with the cover photo of the Statue of Liberty and the designation on the back, "Record Plant, NYC" would lead one to believe otherwise, but this is the session Michael talks about in his tour diary for Pop magazine, an intimate show at the Los Angeles location of The Record Plant, captured through the soundboard.

"Oh, that was awful!" recalls Danny. "Really terrible sound. That *Big Apple Encounters*... the guitar is so out of tune! Just cringy. I can't work it out how. The sound was horrible in those places because we couldn't be loud, you see? We had to be loud." Along with the usual UFO standards at the special gig, the band also hits upon a few rarities, including "Oh My," "Space Child," Willie Dixon's "Built for Comfort" and "All or Nothing" by the Small Faces. In between songs, Phil's acerbic wit is on display in all its terse and deadpanned glory.

"All or Nothing" was used as a bonus track for the 2007 remastered issue of *No Heavy Petting*, but there as also "French Kisses," an oddly poppy and glammy and melodic original, on which Phil sings kind of camp while Michael turns in an extensive twinned lead that is almost pretty. There's also a cover of Frankie Miller's "Have You Seen Me Lately Joan" which is also stylistically quite fixed to the glam boom in Britain fizzling out by 1975. Unsurprisingly, the song is quite pubby, with a bit of a traditional and even Celtic vibe, featuring pervasive strummed acoustic augmented by stabbing electric chords—place this one in a sort of Thin Lizzy zone, just past that band's first two albums into, say, *Vagabonds* and *Nightlife*, signature twin lead included.

Then there's another band original called "Do It if You Can," a simplistic confection of stacked chords, saved somewhat by an action-packed chorus, on which Peyronel is clearly heard. Finally there's "All the Strings," a Queen-like ballad six minutes long, focus on Peyronel and piano and no guitar whatsoever, Schenker's role semi-replaced by Heep-like Hammond. Chord changes-wise, this one evokes Mott the Hoople, and so add it all up, one might say that all the songs not used for *No Heavy Petting*, had they been included instead of some of the others, would have turned the record considerably more glam. Let's not forget, the guys weren't averse to dressing glam either. It's an interesting case of what could have been. All tracks save for "All or Nothing" were recorded at Morgan Studios, along with the songs that made the final record.

Record put to bed and the band back on the road, Michael was always the wild card, as evidenced by an oft-recounted episode deep in the heart of America, this time told by Mr. Peyronel.

"The famous one... you've probably heard it already. It's the one where Schenker... it would always involve Schenker, wouldn't it? It was in the South, in America, Georgia or Kentucky or something like that... In the hotel room during the night, Schenker had trashed the room, so they had called the cops of course. So this typical southern cop comes along, with the mirrored glasses job. Schenker is doing the Nazi salute to the guy, going, 'You fucking Hitler!' 'Sieg Heil, come on, arrest me, you bastard, you cunt.' (laughs). I wasn't there when it happened, but I can just imagine the copper going 'Alright, let's go... come with me, sonny.'"

"So they take him to the police station, and we have to do a big stadium show in Flint, Michigan. So we went to the police station, and we convinced the manager of the hotel to not press charges. We paid the bill, 'Send us the bill or whatever, don't press charges.' So we go to the cop shop to get him, and they come back and say, 'Sorry, he's going to have to stay.' Because he'd pulled the sanitary facilities from the cell, pulled them off the wall and smashed them up. We're all going, oh no and we missed the gig. We couldn't do that Flint thing. I think we had to stay another night and pay 500 bucks or more, 1,500 maybe. It was just a disaster. So at that point, we thought, okay, fuck it. Let's get his girlfriend over and see if that can control him. Which is exactly what happened. She came over and she was a lovely girl, German girl, very, very nice girl. We flew her over and that was the end of that. He was like a monk. Wouldn't drink, nothing. We should have done this in the first place. Much cheaper."

Asked if Michael was always like that, trashing hotel rooms and the like, Danny says, "No, never. I mean, not on the tours I did with him. He'd never done that. He just... he'd be with two girls at the same time or something, or in the corridor running like a madman and shouting, 'Hey pussy cunts, come to me; come pussy cunts!' Which was funny, but no, he didn't break anything. Not until then."

But after a whack of touring, Danny's tenure in the band would draw to a close. "I was out at the end of '76, I believe. But I don't know, I was really excited about the band. I remember phoning Pete and saying something like, after the second tour, 'I guess this is not right and that is not right but we can fix those things. I've got some great ideas for songs. We're going to do a great album!' I was really enthusiastic. And with hindsight, I could tell that Pete probably knew already that they were gonna sack me (laughs). Because he sounded totally, 'Oh yeah, yeah, Dan, sure.' Which was a shame. But then, with hindsight, when it was all finished, I probably also gave out that at the same time, that I really wasn't going to be staying long. I don't know, it's difficult to say. You can't really analyse these things."

"I don't really think that my departure from the band was anything other than political, because musically, it seemed to be working," muses Danny. "We got along pretty well, not incredible, but normally. We didn't have any big fights. So I think it was a political thing. Because the album didn't reach the... Chrysalis thought this was going to be the big breakthrough album, because *Force It* had made it into the Top 50 or something. The album didn't live up to that reputation, success-wise. But you and I know perfectly well, that that doesn't mean that the keyboard player needs to be sacked (laughs). There could've been a million factors, or several factors. It could've been that the company didn't do their job right. Or the moment wasn't right for the release. The album sounded good, and in fact, many people are rediscovering it. It was just political; it happens. They needed somebody to blame. 'Oh, get rid of him.' Who knows?"

So yes, tension was palpable, indicates Michael. "I remember one thing that Phil said when we did *No Heavy Petting*, he said, like, 'This should be it. If this isn't going to be it, I'm out of here. I'm out of the music business.' So obviously he was desperate to make it, and the next album turned out to be it. So probably, for his sake, he was lucky that he didn't stop then (laughs)."

Danny shows surprise at Michael's comment. "Really? Wow, maybe that's why they gave in to the pressure. Because they themselves felt a bit desperate, maybe. I didn't really know that. It's very kind of schizophrenic, my whole thing with Phil. We certainly weren't friends. We weren't enemies. As I say, he didn't hit me, for instance, as he did many other musicians in the band. He never even attempted to. So I guess relatively speaking, we got on pretty well (laughs). But I remember that at the time, I didn't really think much of his vocals, and certainly of his stage presence. With the years, I have to tell you that I completely changed my mind, and now I think he is easily one of the greatest rock singers, or R&B singers more like, in the sense that... one grows up and one learns what really makes a great singer and what doesn't, you know? His voice is just so particular. You know immediately it's him. Like David Gilmour on guitar. So I think I really judged him badly or underestimated him. I still don't think he's that great onstage, his presence, but he's a fucking great singer. That's good enough for me. But I don't know. I didn't feel that they felt it was the end, no."

Pete adds clarity to the situation. "The funny thing was that Chrysalis had just gone from Warner Brothers to go independent. Ironically enough, that's exactly why that album didn't do well. Because it wasn't in the shops. The next album, *Lights Out*, went straight into the Top 30. That's all it was. It had nothing to do with Danny at all. But I have to say, when actually onstage, I don't really worry about keyboards. They're like, well, if you put the keyboards in the car park that would be lovely. But yes, Chrysalis became their own label in America at that point, but ironically, down the line, the album still sells. We were going to tour with Kiss and we didn't do the tour because the album had not gone into the charts, as we were expecting. It didn't follow up *Force It* the same way, ironically enough, because as I say, it was because the actual albums weren't in the shops. We were caught in the label thing. Therefore, the proof of the pudding was when *Lights Out* came out. It wasn't that much better, particularly, than *No Heavy Petting*. It was just that it was in the shops! That's true."

"Danny fit in fine," is Leo's comment on the situation. "I mean, Danny had aspirations to write too, and that may have been frustrating for him. I didn't get into arguments with the band or even discussions with the band as to what or who took credit for what. Golly, I was in a band myself where I could get into those arguments (laughs). It was very difficult. In a way, I championed UFO with the record company because they just thought well, they'll sell a few records in Germany. You know, our first release in the states charted and caught everyone by surprise. The boss of the record company said, 'Oh, congratulations, we've got hit.' I spoke to the regional A&R manager and he said 'Oh, it won't get any further.' I said, 'Why not?' 'Well, because we haven't shipped enough.' You know probably better than I do how it works in the States. If it's not in the stores, they don't buy it. If they aren't selling it, the radio doesn't play it. But yes, the album was under-shipped and under-promoted."

Ironically, Leo's answer mirrors Danny's, with respect to why Leo wasn't around for the next UFO record. Reflects Lyons, "It was basically because the record company thought, well, we've missed out on these three, but we really need an American hit, so we better put some money into it and hire an American producer. I'm sure it was the policy with a lot of companies but it certainly was with Chrysalis at the time. They thought, right, we'll get an American producer because we need an American hit on the radio. I don't think it was necessarily my fault or the band's that those first three records... I mean, they did sell; they were successful. If you hit Soundscan now—or as I did, back when it first came out—and you look at UFO's career, all the records have done about the same number. But obviously the profile was raised by record company investment. I mean, it happens all the time. I hate to think I was complaining about it. It's just unfortunate that the company weren't behind the spontaneity of certainly the first two records, if not the third, which charted, got airplay and started to happen. I mean, that's something you can't buy. Usually, you have to spend a lot of money so you can get that far, and that happens spontaneously. So if they had been able to service the records, I think it would've been a different thing for the band's career."

"The interesting thing is," continues Lyons, "maybe by the time they had reached their fifth record, which I didn't do, they actually asked me to manage them, which I did for a short period of time. Then there was a rift (laughs). It was such a brief period of time though. I took the band, talked to them, told them what I thought they should do. I had very definite ideas of what I thought they should do from a career point of view. One of them was to get out of debt. I looked at what their position was with the record company and renegotiated their recording deal with them. Because they were on such a terrible deal with Chrysalis Records at the time, the first huge successful record that they would have had, there would have been no money. So we renegotiated that. But then I told the guys they had to tighten the belts a little bit and be realistic about how they were working, and gave them an ultimatum, and they decided not to take my ultimatum (laughs). So I only managed them maybe for a few weeks, in the interim period. I mean, subsequently of course, I have spoken to the band over the years since then and they did say, 'Bloody 'ell, I wish we'd listened!' (laughs). Like a lot of bands, they don't really know when they're blowing money on limos and hotels, that in the end it's their money."

"I do know one thing," opines Danny, in closing, "and that's just from a musical point of view, from just listening to the stuff... for years I didn't listen to the UFO stuff anymore; I was doing my thing. But somebody gave me a greatest hits thing, and it had a lot of the newer stuff on there, and I have to say that a lot of the newer stuff seemed to go in the same direction we started with when I was in the band. It's weird. One has to draw one's own conclusions."

Chapter Seven
Lights Out

"It was luxurious and fun, the bar open every night"

Starving for a hit by this point, UFO soldiered on, replacing Danny Peyronel with ex-Savoy Brown keyboardist Paul "Kipper" Raymond, who, crucially, could also pitch in with rhythm guitar when called upon. Little did the band know that they had added another vital writer to the team, even if Raymond, for contractual reasons, would have to be kept off the credits for the time being.

Raymond had come up through the rock 'n' roll ranks, debuting at the age of 22 with Plastic Penny in 1967 and then replacing none other than Christine Perfect (later McVie) in Chicken Shack. Next was Savoy Brown, from where Paul would make the jump to UFO. Paul had come to the attention of UFO when Savoy Brown were the sandwich band between an opening UFO and a headlining Nazareth in Saginaw, Michigan. Pete Way had watched the Savoy set, in which Paul and Kim Simmonds traded off lead vocals and Paul played, adeptly in the eyes of Pete, both keyboards and guitar. He had mentioned to Paul that they were thinking of replacing Danny Peyronel, and back in the UK, drinks, dinner and a perfunctory audition were set up, after which Paul was in.

In any event, whether it was due to luck or skill or the fresh blood slaked through the arrival of Paul, UFO found themselves firing on all sixes, bounding into AIR Studios in London, February and March 1977, with a new producer in Ron Nevison, mix to follow at Pye Studios. The result would be the hit record that had thus far eluded them, *Lights Out* rising to No.54 in the UK charts and No.23 in

America. Oddly, the band had never reached such heights, despite a string of strong, potentially album-catapulting anthems such as "Rock Bottom," "Doctor Doctor," "Let It Roll," "Shoot Shoot," "Natural Thing" and "Highway Lady" to their credit. In fact, the band now had three solid albums under their belts (to add to three dodgy ones).

Remarked Andy, back in 1977 to Way Ahead magazine, "Danny didn't quite fit in. You've got to understand when you're being pushed to work, to try to find a person is a very difficult thing. You don't get much time to fit them in and get out on the road. Living with people 24 hours a day is an awful strain. I mean, I've been with Pete for seven years. Michael's been with us for over three years. To take people in is very difficult, because you're kind of forced together. It's just that Danny didn't fit in."

On the other hand... "Paul seems to be very, very good," says Parker. "As a person we get on really well and apart from that, he plays keyboards and guitars and sings, which is a great boon. Keyboard players are okay, but you know, this band thrives on two guitar work as well, so it's nice if you've got the kind of laid-back aspect of the keyboards, because they are basically more of a background thing. It's nice if you've got that and you can have the guitar work as well; it's a good mixture."

For just that reason, with the arrival of Paul Raymond, UFO became even more of an explosive force live. On the subject of meshing with Michael Schenker, when both happened to be playing guitar, Raymond says the arrangement worked well because, "I play the strings from the other way up. So it's more of a brighter sound. Michael has said that of all the guitarists he's played with, mine complemented his the best. That's what he told me and Barry as well, so he must mean it." The Barry to which Paul refers, is bassist Barry Sparks, who had worked with Michael in MSG as well as having toured with UFO in America in 2004, after visa problems left Pete Way back in England.

"So yeah, it's because I play upside down," clarifies Raymond. "So a lot of times, I play like Keith Richards, stroking up, to sort of compensate, on the bass strings. But it still has a bright sound, because I play down most of this time. That seems to complement his style."

"I don't have any malice for the man," muses Paul, reflecting in the early 2000s on this era with Michael. "He's a very talented man and we're still playing all those songs, which he co-wrote. I would like to think that... well, Pete said this in an interview recently, that we wouldn't rule out the possibility that Michael might play with us again—it could almost happen. It's just whenever he feels he wants to do it. But he's very difficult to work with. For *Lights Out* and *Obsession*, Michael was always out there on his own, naturally, because his English wasn't that good anyway and he's a bit reclusive, which I do understand. You know, if you don't speak a language that well, you do tend to withdraw. That classic line-up, it was perfect."

"With Danny Peyronel on *No Heavy Petting*, it wasn't quite right," continues Raymond, "because he was only a keyboard player. Danny had a good voice, but it still wasn't right. When Pete approached me to join the band, I think that is the defining moment, the turning point, that this other person in the group would double on guitar and do keyboards, and was a writer too. I think everybody had their role. Pete was the showman; he sells the band. Michael was very, very good-looking and an idol guitarist; I think he was one-of-a-kind at that time. Certainly when he left, it was a terrible job replacing him. Eddie Van Halen said he saw the ad, and he said he didn't think he was good enough to replace Michael. Plus living in Pasadena at the time, he had his own band playing locally. Anyway, I suppose he wouldn't have been right for us anyway."

"It's always been 60% guitar, because it's a guitar-based band and the keyboards are the frills," answers Paul, asked about the split between the two solitudes. "And that's where Danny... you know, because Danny didn't have anything to do. So he tried to play along with the guitar riffs, and it just didn't sound right, with the piano. You've got to have two guitars sometimes."

Starting with the outer wrap, *Lights Out* sported another good one. "That's Michael and Phil," says Pete Way. "That was at Battersea Station in London; Hipgnosis did it. They would look at what you'd got and often they would see something in it and they would go from there. They were very interesting people to work with because they were very innovative. I mean they did Zeppelin stuff, Floyd, interesting things."

Michael Schenker picks up the story. "With *Lights Out*, we ended up in that factory, where Pink Floyd had that pig floating in the air on *Animals*. We went into the Power Station and all I knew was to put on these overalls and show one shoulder. I had no clue what they were up to but then later on people were talking about it, and I realised what the idea was. But it was kind of weird. I was really never involved in that. We had a really good team that was doing the album artwork, and Phil was pretty good when it came down to concepts and lyrics and stuff. He comes up with unusual stuff. Between them and him, it always turned out good. I don't think people liked the monkey too much on *No Heavy Petting* (laughs). I think people weren't connecting too well with that. But other than that, the artwork became a pretty important part of UFO."

Noted Phil, speaking with Geoff Barton, "Two males—or are they males?—are standing about, one in the foreground, the other in the background, undressing, his overalls down around his waist. You can add your own interpretation; it's another one of those."

Opening this strident, grand, perhaps slightly more melodic album was a crashing, bashing pub rocker called "Too Hot to Handle." Immediately the listener fell into a good vibe, not unlike that occasionally broached by UFO sister band Thin Lizzy.

"It's just a simple riff I had," explains Pete, "which is almost like Grand Funk's "American Band" or something like that; it has that feel to it. My part within UFO is that I tend to write more of the rock things, things that Michael doesn't normally touch. It's one of those things; my whole attitude towards music tends to go to the live side of things, so there is always an energy in it. In those days—and this might seem strange—we used to go to the pub and come back from the pub and play things, if I've got an idea or Michael's got an idea. It wasn't like nowadays with the new albums, where we come in and say, 'This is my idea for the song; it starts like this, goes like that.' In those days, there was a good chemistry there. I'm not saying there isn't in the new stuff, because you always find a way back to the chemistry; you just adapt it. But in those days it was very much a touring band and I think that came into the way that particular song came across."

"'Too Hot to Handle' is a straight Pete Way riff," affirms Phil. "You couldn't get more simple than that. That's just a straight, 'Hey, look, I found a D and E chord!' That was a dead-easy one (laughs). So that's just a straight me and Pete, and then we bludgeoned Michael into playing it." Phil's lyric on this one ain't much either, even if a few decent if frustratingly succinct lines emerge.

"Just Another Suicide" is like a fragile, poppier, maybe less inspired version of *No Heavy Petting*'s "Highway Lady." It bounces along to the strains of acoustic guitar, elegant piano, even strings, courtesy of producer Ron Nevison, hot from engineering work for Bad Company, The Who and Led Zeppelin. "That was actually Paul Raymond's riff," notes Pete. "It reminds me of that Jackson Browne song, 'Running on Empty,' and I did that type of bass on it. Actually it was Paul's lyrics too, as a matter of fact (note: Paul agrees—"that song was all me"). But I think due to some sort of publishing thing—I think Paul had gotten an advance of somebody else's—he didn't get credit, but it was actually Paul's lyrics on that. I think it was very much his song whilst performed by the band." The considerably involved, quite sympathetic and convincing lyric marks the painful thought process from original despair through to suicide, resulting in a considerable contrast between music and word.

"Phil paints a picture, doesn't he?" says Paul. "Not so much now, but back in the day. I was listening to the old records and listening to... how does he come up with all these great lyrics? Where does he get his inspiration from? So yes, to a certain extent he does have an influence on me. When I worked in Savoy Brown, we worked in a totally different way. I came into UFO and saw this new way of working, working up a backing track first and then somebody writing something to it. But with Savoy Brown, we'd start with the lyrics, actually, and then make music to it; I think Elton John works that way. Whatever you're comfortable with. So yeah, Phil really, he is one of the best, definitely."

"I believe he's covered two of my songs, in thirty something years," chuckles Paul. "Or is it three? The first of mine he took on was 'Just Another Suicide,' which I actually open my solo live set with. That's a song that's never been gigged. The second one was 'Take It or Leave It,' which I've also put in my live set, which was from *No Place to Run*. Then the third one was just recently, on the *You Are Here* album, a song called 'Sympathy' on there. He took that one on board, because it's very much in his style. If you write it in his style, then he'll sing it. But if it turns out Paul McCartney, then he won't (laughs)."

Asked if he'd take on the responsibility of having brought a Queen-like flourish to UFO, Paul says, "Maybe. They had a record out back in the '70s called *News of the World*, and that really was my favourite Queen album. UFO had a guitarist that sounded a little bit like Brian May. I don't know; very different sorts of bands, really. They're more operatic, aren't they?"

Phil doesn't quite recall the hubbub over Paul's legal status in the band. "Vaguely, I think there was something to do with 'Another Suicide,' and I think 'Ain't No Baby' on *Obsession* was his riff. But I think it got sorted out in the end. There was something going on and it was just a lot easier to save any long-running problem to put down whoever's there and sort it out later."

Phil goes on to explain the difference between a song from Pete and one from Paul. "Pete's a two-to three-chord man, more of a feel, and Paul would tend to be structured, if sometimes a little over-structured. So we take out a little bit of the structure and we've got a Paul number."

As important as the arrival of Paul Raymond to the band is the arrival of aforementioned storied producer Ron Nevison, who will be on board for the duration of the '70s, for the band's biggest record, *Lights Out*, plus *Obsession*, plus the well-regarded decade-closing double live album *Strangers in the Night*.

As Nevison explains in conversation with Jeb Wright, he was already a British ex-pat of sorts set up in sunny Los Angeles, but he went back to England to produce *Lights Out* at the venerable Air Studios.

"In 1975 I decided to come to LA for a number of reasons. I built a studio for Ronnie Wood at his house. The Faces were doing a tour of LA and the Record Plant mobile was recording the shows. Ronnie Lane and Woody were friends with the guys at the Record Plant and they invited them over to England. I was doing a session in Ronnie's studio at his house. I met them and they knew I had done The Who and that I had done Bad Company and they offered me a job on the spot to be the chief engineer at the Record Plant in LA. I didn't take it immediately, but I took it eventually."

"There were a lot of people leaving England at that time due to the Labour government who closed all of the tax loopholes. Rod Stewart moved to LA, the Stones moved to France, Elton John moved to LA. A lot of people were leaving because they were taxing people on out of the country earnings. If you stayed in England more than 63 days a year, then you were subject to taxes on anything you earned anywhere in the world. Everyone was leaving and I had a job offer in LA so I took it. The final straw for me was when they offered me a house in Beverly Hills where I could live. They rented me a house. I moved there and of course, at that time The Record Plant had three studios in LA and two studios in Sausalito where I am now."

"I used to shuttle back and forth when I wasn't doing sessions and just oversee all of the engineers and assistants," continues Nevison. "After a while I decided to leave, not because I didn't like the job, but because I couldn't work anywhere else. I had big clients that told me they wanted me, but they didn't want to work at The Record Plant. Not everybody liked The Record Plant. They didn't like the sound or whatever. I decided that I was doing well enough that I should go independent and I've been independent ever since. That was probably in 1977. I still worked at The Record Plant a lot, but if somebody wanted me to come to London to work, which UFO did, then I could do that. I did *Lights Out* in 1977 and I couldn't have done that if I was still tied into the job. It was a time-consuming job being a chief engineer of a major studio."

"So unfortunately, I did a bunch of albums with UFO," laughs Nevison, in an earlier interview with the author. "I did four albums with them, three in the '70s and then *Walk on Water* in 1995. UFO suffered from the fact that they were on the Chrysalis label, where Chrysalis did not have distribution in this country. They were just independent, but we had plenty of radio airplay. So everybody loved UFO but we didn't sell a lot of records. Because Chrysalis didn't really come into their own until Blondie and Pat Benatar came along, later, after the five albums I did with Chrysalis, including two Babys albums. That's another five albums that I did in the '70s, from British rockers, on top of Zeppelin and Bad Company. But yes, The Babys had lots of radio success. I did have a lot of success with them also but they just couldn't sell the records."

"*Lights Out* was much more orchestrated than the second one, *Obsession*," continues Nevison. "Everybody loved it; I thought it was great. The band wasn't sure, initially, but the response to the album was overwhelmingly great. I mean, I had a standing ovation when I brought the record back to Chrysalis and played it for Terry Ellis in the boardroom and his staff. That was incredible for me. They realised where UFO was with their previous four or five albums, and where they were now, and they saw that instantly. I used a lot of orchestrations and I didn't use as many on *Obsession*. Clearly everybody's favourite album is either *Lights Out* or *Obsession*, that they ever did—I'm proud of that."

Asked to compare working with Andy Parker as opposed to Thin Lizzy's Brian Downey or Bad Company's Simon Kirke or John

Bonham, Ron figures, "Well you can't compare anybody to John Bonham; it's not comparable. But he did a good job. He and Pete Way were not the world's greatest rhythm section, but it was UFO—which had the world's greatest guitar player. That's all it needed. The rest of them, Phil Mogg was not the world's greatest singer, but we had a great guitar player who also was one of the main writers in the band. He wrote the guitar riffs, but his biggest problem that I had found, which I couldn't do anything about, was that he did not write with the band. He didn't write for vocals."

"It's something I never really consciously worked on," reflects Andy, asked if there is an Andy Parker percussion sound or style. "I never went out with a game and planned to come out with an Andy Parker sound. I just listened to people. I always loved the drum kits, like Cozy Powell's, another Ludwig player—isn't that strange? I liked John Bonham, with that big, fat sound with the space around it. As much as I admire these technicians, these guys who could play really fast, it doesn't float my boat. I'm kind of like your Dave Gilmour of guitar players. I like two notes where others would play twenty; that's better for me, just more my thing."

"But John Bonham, I just kind of like his style that no one really uses, that syncopation with his hands, between his snare drum—I just love that kind of stuff. I don't know, for twenty-odd years I've basically tried to play as loud as I could. I'm not quite as loud as I used to be, but it was a struggle, to make yourself heard. So I kind of tuned the kit to sound as good as possible, and I just hit the things as hard as I could with the biggest sticks I could manage. Now, these days it's not quite the same. There's a more relaxed feeling in the band, and everyone has kind of moved on. So now I don't struggle so hard to make myself heard. I still play loud, and as I'm getting my chops back, the volume is coming back as well, because it's not as hard to play loud for a long time. But for me, it's just getting a nice big fat sound and just trying to be heard, really. I'm just not one for chops. I'm sort of between John Bonham and Phil Rudd (laughs). I love Phil; he doesn't even need any tom-toms, does he? And you don't miss them."

"So I had to rearrange everything to accommodate the vocals," continues Nevison, back on the conundrum of working with the boys. "Phil Mogg was a really, really fine lyricist, but he took forever to write. Which is fine. But I had working titles for songs. I had to kind of do the entire production without any lyrics, in some cases. Which is difficult, to try and figure out what this song is about and to try to make it musically work. In the end he always came through, but I'm talking literally the day of the final vocal, and he's still fucking with the lyrics. So it was a little bit difficult, in so much as we had these really anthemic kind of great things that Schenker was coming up with, but they weren't arranged in any kind of logical... in fact nothing about Schenker was logical. So they weren't arranged. I had to kind of break them down and make them into verse/chorus, verse/chorus."

Illustrative of that point, Ron explains that, "I remember a song called 'Try Me' on the *Lights Out* album, that Terry Ellis wanted to release as a single. He said it doesn't have any form. I said, you should've heard it before, you know? I made it into a song. It had great solos and great things, but we had a real challenge. But I think it got a little easier once we got past the *Lights Out* album. For *Obsession* it got a little easier to go in and reconstruct Schenker's riffs into songs. Still, the conversations I had with him were in broken German English. 'I want my guitar to be accurate.' Well, what is accurate? It means he wants it in tune. Accurate, okay. Yeah, and if you can imagine a German kid working with English kids, who are taking this out on him, needling him about the war and all that shit. It was pretty hilarious to tell you the truth (laughs). We had a strained relationship a little bit. I mean, he was a good sport. He was off to the movies and doing this and that. It was tough to keep them together at times."

Back to the running order of *Lights Out*, the aforementioned "Try Me" is an even softer music for the band, Phil crooning over a spare piano line and creeping strings. "I mean, that was good, wasn't it?" queries Pete. "The sound of the lead, a really nice solo, the orchestra thing; and it was a live orchestra too. This was before people used keyboards for that. But it was an expensive album for the fact that we did use live stuff, and we did indeed bring the orchestra to Air Studios. Ron came into it and he added production into it."

Continues Pete, "I think the hard rock songs... he let things like 'Too Hot to Handle' be raw, but he gave it an overall bigger sound. Actually, we always wanted the Led Zeppelin drum sound, because he was the engineer on *Physical Graffiti*. But it was kind of smoothed-out for American radio. Unfortunately, at that point in time, we kind of resented smoothing stuff out too much. But unfortunately, to a certain extent then, we went after Top 30 singles. America and Canada, they liked to hear that kind of thing, didn't they? I also remember that Phil would be there doing the vocals with Ron. Ron was very, very challenging as a guy who works on vocals and he would give you a hard time. Sometimes you didn't really hear what was going on though. I wouldn't be there at every stage other than doing my bass. Phil would then come up with the ideas for melodies and things. Or Michael would do something and Phil would go, 'Hey, that would be good for me to sing over.'"

"I listened to the albums that they had done previously and they were just rock albums and they all sounded the same" comments Ron, asked about the further challenge of massaging string arrangements into these records. "They didn't stand out to me in any particular fashion. At this point in 1977, as a producer, there wasn't anything available to a producer. There weren't any synthesizers to speak of. Of course there was, and I just worked with a genius, which was Pete Townshend, at that time, in the early '70s, with the new ARP 2600, but there wasn't really anything you could use. We had a B3, a Fender Rhodes, a Wurlitzer, an acoustic piano—that's about it."

"I wanted to do something special on this album, and so I talked to the people at Chrysalis, and I had worked in the early '70s, a year or two before that, I had done an album with Flo and Eddie called *Moving Targets*. I'm not sure how I got hooked up with this guy, but I got hooked up with a Canadian in Toronto named Alan McMillan, who, if I remember correctly—and I still talk to Alan occasionally—I think that he had done some stuff for Alice Cooper, with that Canadian producer, Bob Ezrin. They asked me if I would use this guy and I said yes, if he can do like rock, like Alice Cooper stuff for Flo and Eddie, that would be great."

"He came down and he blew me away. I put him up in the Sunset Marquis and he wrote away and it blew me away. So when I thought of somebody to come over and do the orchestrations for what I wanted to do on two or three or four UFO songs, he came over, and again blew me away. Then I had them on The Babys too. So that kind of period of time, late '70s, Alan McMillan was my go-to guy, and he did a great job on The Babys' *Broken Heart* album, UFO *Lights Out*, and the Flo and Eddie album called *Moving Targets*. I don't know if he did any more albums with me than those three, but possibly."

"Ron liked it his way," says Andy, asked to recall the working relationship. "But it's interesting, back in the day we were a handful, don't forget. We were pretty wild back when Ron was dealing with us. It was interesting, because Leo was a lot easier-going. Leo was our first big producer. He came in and did the first three Chrysalis albums and he did a great job. But he was really, really good. He would come to rehearsals and he would record it all and go away and think about it and come back with ideas. Which is what we really needed. But I think in the end, we were kind of getting crazier and Leo was probably not a firm enough hand for us. So I think it's probably why... I can't remember who actually came up with the decision to switch to get Nevison in, but put it this way, at the time Ron came in, it's kind of what we needed. Because we were getting a bit crazy."

"It's the chemistry," answers Schenker, asked to articulate how Nevison had inspired him. "It's not something you analyse or something you know what it is or whatever. It is what it is. If people could analyse exactly what it is, you could put a book together on the successful chemistry. It doesn't exist, it can't be done, it's impossible. It's a deeper-rooted spiritual aspect that we don't understand. You have the chemistry or you don't. You can put both instruments together and it might not turn out very well. It just has to be complementary; everybody complements everybody and puts all the missing parts in. It's a quality that each member of that team had, that would combine to a kind of phenomenon, as I can see it."

But this was clearly a fecund period for Michael. "Yes, when I started making my first record, every next record was an amazing development, all the way up to *Lovedrive*. Basically, the period where I did develop, in those few years, developed so fast; what happened to me was always from one album to the next, an incredible step. The early UFO until 1979; that was a very definite kind of step-by-step musical development."

"With the Scorpions I did my first record ever, and with UFO, my first album with an English band, and the second album was a step forward in a way that I can't really explain, but it was a step in-between; *Force It* and *Phenomenon* were basically getting ready for *Lights Out*, kind of thing. So you step forward every year, every one-and-a-half years. Ron Nevison was the next step, but also Paul Raymond coming in, another missing link that made everything more complete. Every step was an incredible improvement. Then by the time I came to 1979 and did *Lovedrive* with the Scorpions, which worked out pretty good, then it was time to focus on other aspects.

So that's what I did. I learned so much. All the things that I didn't see before I started to see, and then I experienced things that I didn't even know were there (laughs). It's amazing, but I guess that's my custom-made journey, like every person has their own custom-made journey going. Mine just worked out with those kinds of extremes."

"'Try Me' was done on my Revox," notes Michael, as we turn back again to *Lights Out*. "This was the reel-to-reel I had in those days. In fact, you know the opening to 'Love to Love,' or was it that one? I can't even remember now. Because I used it in a different spot live. I did something on a Revox; it was on a two-track, but it bounced back and forth, back and forth, as many times as you wanted. So it could become like six or seven or eight tracks, but you'd lose some things. Oh wait, maybe it was even an echo thing I used to have, that used to run with the tape. You could put a lot of things on this tape, but at some point, what you started with would appear again; you can add things to it. I think I did something on that or the Revox. I'd put something together that I wasn't able to reproduce in a studio. So we used that particular tape that I did in my bedroom on a very, very amateur type of level. But somehow it had so much atmosphere, it was impossible to reproduce. It was totally by accident, or wasn't something that was planned. 'Try Me' was something I did on that same tape recorder, which is basically an instrumental piece, and then we added the vocals around the instrumental piece."

"I was writing songs that were always instrumentals in the first place," said Michael, speaking with John Stix about this idea of building songs without vocals in mind. "Then the singer put something in front and something behind it. I was writing so many instrumentals, I could've made instrumental albums. That's how I started writing. 'Try Me' was an instrumental. I gave it to Phil and said, 'What do you think of this?' He told me where if I left the guitars out, he could sing to it. Sometimes it was better to keep the instrumental part as a lead break and write something heavier for the front and end because the lead break was more romantic. Sometimes by leaving off the lead guitars and using the rhythm guitars, there were still enough chords, and it was good enough for the vocalist to sing to and then go into the instrumental. Then I had the more rock songs, where I was improvising and using ten different tracks and putting lead break after lead break. If there were too many good things on each one and I couldn't decide, then I just stitched them together."

Yes, stitch together everything that Pete and Ron and Michael has said about song writing and you begin to understand the challenge, and, arguably, why it was hard to get hits out of UFO. To boil it down, Michael has admitted that essentially he writes instrumentals. Phil then is very last minute with his lyrics. Somebody, basically a combination now of Ron and Phil, at the final hour, has to work out the mechanics of vocal phrasing and melody. What results is that some pretty heavy lifting has to get done at the vocal booth stage and what goes down on tape is a song that has not had time to gestate, to steep, to be displayed and played against any sort of band debate on it.

"I helped fill out the verses on that," adds Paul, referring to "Try Me." "I gave him a vocal melody, which I think I stole from Free, but I don't think that anybody noticed (laughs). I love 'Try Me.' I think Phil's vocal on that one... whoa, Tony Bennett, eat your heart out (laughs)."

Smashing the calm of "Try Me" is side one closer "Lights Out," soon to be ranked with "Doctor Doctor" and "Rock Bottom" in the trinity of UFO anthems. "The song 'Lights Out' was actually a tough one," notes Ron. "It's fast, and it's hard to get guitars to articulate when they are that fast. But there were keyboards, and I remember Paul, who is a lovely guy, when we were doing 'Lights Out,' I said to him, 'Paul, we are going to have to do your part over after the tracking.' He said, 'Why?' I said, 'You're making a lot of mistakes.' He said, 'Why do I have to be playing with the tracks then?' I told him, 'If you're not playing, then somebody is going to creep into your part.' If he was not there, then someone else will play more and there would not be room for his part when we wanted to put it back on. He said, 'Okay.' He couldn't argue with that."

Adds Pete: "Well, that was a rocker, wasn't it? It was almost like our punk thing." Yet the song was too aristocratic, too buoyant to be deemed anything close to punk, although some of those melodies were dripping with all things British, which perhaps, necessarily includes punk. As well, the track evokes similar sentiments to Thin Lizzy bookends "Jailbreak" and "The Boys Are Back in Town," its music regal, its lyric obliquely warning of violent urban crime to come.

"Actually, that was also co-written with Pete," explains Schenker. "He had the main riff and then I wrote the rest of it. I remember being in the studio mixing and it was very exciting. It was the first album we did with a great producer. We did the three albums before with Leo Lyons and then that was our big step, doing the *Lights Out* album with Ron Nevison. Everything just went up, like 100%. The songs were really good, and plus we had just found Paul Raymond so we had a very, very good chemistry between the producer and Paul and the band, etc. It was the most, how would you say, complete UFO album."

"'Lights Out' is really an aggressive number," said Phil, on the press trail at the time, speaking with Circus. "The lyrics are aggressive. It's the kind of thing that's going on in London at the moment. This whole movement, this whole aggression thing that's really sweeping the country. 'Lights Out' is the epitome of that. I think this album condenses the better moments from a lot of our other albums. It is more accessible than the other ones. A lot of people have gotten into it who hadn't liked UFO before. The production is a lot crisper and up. These songs reflect the current mood we're in."

Side two opened with an unravelling sort of pop rocker called "Gettin' Ready," the relaxed flipside of "Too Hot to Handle" perhaps. Then we got a cover, "Alone Again Or," once more, nicely augmented with strings, in addition to brass. Ron Nevison was proud of his work on this one, as well as Alan McMillan's orchestration, calling UFO's version "beautiful" and "a new beginning for UFO." It had been Ron's idea to include a cover on the album, but Phil picked this specific track. The idea to include strings met with some resistance from the band, but Nevison got his way, and perhaps also more than he bargained for, with the process taking a week.

Pete picks up the story. "We chose that because we liked that band Love and the album, and we just wanted to do something off that album. There were another couple of songs of that nature that we thought about. What was funny is that it got played in California a lot because obviously that's a Californian band. But I think it was one of the things that gave the album some depth. I can't remember the other songs we were thinking about. There were several of them. But I think Ron thought yeah, that would be good. It worked out good, because, where it was done by a horn section in Love, Michael did the lead with guitar and gave it that melody. We just adapted it good."

"The saxophone solo, I mean, I listened to it and I went, what can I do with this?" adds Michael. "In those days I had my pedals specialized to a certain sweet sound and it was perfect for that solo. So it worked out. It was kind of a strange song, to be honest, for UFO to do. Because it kind of sticks out like a sore thumb; it's different. It's not a typical UFO thing. It's a good question. I don't even know why we ended up doing it (laughs). But I guess the producer probably convinced us."

UFO's version would eventually be swept aside by that of punk heroes The Damned, who would cover the song in 1987 and score a substantial UK hit with their equally sincere telling. It was just as odd for The Damned to be covering it as well, even though Dave Vanian and the boys were into their gothic phase, and the guys had always been huge '60s rock aficionados.

"We wanted to put a number that wasn't written by the band on the album," said Phil at the time, speaking with Geoff Barton, "and we've always liked 'Alone Again Or,' so we decided to do it. In the end, however, when I listened to the completed record, I wasn't so sure. I said that I had one or two reservations, and that might be one of them. I can't help but come to the conclusion that this band can't do other people's numbers."

Second to last on the record was a leaden rocker called "Electric Phase." It is in fact a slow song made highly interesting through its electric weaves, its arrangement, its band chemistry. Phil's lyric examines electric connection first through the phone line and then through face-to-face chemistry. Bottom line, it's the best lyric on the album, for, amusingly, given all the things Phil could write about with a title like that, it's about telephone wires.

"I think I came up with that riff at rehearsal," notes Pete, "after coming out of the pub, and then Michael came in with his melody part. Like I say, we used to get ready for the rehearsal, go to the pub, come back and kind of jam ideas. When I say jam, we used to put parts into the songs a lot more in those days. It was sort of like having fun. Yeah, we always stuck to the pub that was closest (laughs), the quickest to get to. It was good because you can just get out of the studio, get something to eat and something to drink. We tended to work sort of more mid-afternoon until one or two in the morning. It wasn't late night sessions. Sometimes it would go on, but I think more with the band, it depends who you're working with. I think Ron used to do with Led Zeppelin some really, really late night stuff and I think he found that, with us, he liked to stick to banker's hours, because of his hearing and that."

"Yeah, that was done by Pete," affirms Michael, with respect to

"Electric Phase." "I think he had that part when we were in the rehearsal studio and then I kind of immediately went, there is something missing, because it just went like (sings it); there was really nothing there. I said, there is some melody missing. So I just added this whole melodic part behind it and the combination of this very staccato-like riff, and then it went, almost like a wave, into the melody and it really added a nice contrast and made a nice song."

Finally, closing out the album was, fittingly, the record's set piece, "Love to Love," a long, moody epic with all sorts of UFO magic at every turn, Phil enigmatic with his lost love poetry. A piano ballad, a progressive rocker, a coat hanger for yet more strings, a hard rock juggernaut at times... this is perhaps the band's crowning moment. "I like doing it live," opines Pete. "I think it's a great song. It was interesting; Michael would come up with the melody and I guess we jammed around the melody and we put the sort of hard front thing in, which now reminds me of Metallica or something like that, then into that melody thing. I really enjoy doing it because it's got so much scope, so much depth. I like the melodies on that."

Paul Raymond gives Ron Nevison part credit for the success of "Love to Love"—the song is Nevison's favourite on the album—but says, "he's a bit of a taskmaster, not the easiest guy to work with. He thinks he gets the best out of people by being really insulting to them. But he gets the job done. I don't know if he ever spoke to Paul Rodgers as badly as he did to us (laughs). But yeah, the ends justify the means. Also, he helped us turn a page, because not only did I just join the band and it was my first album, but he added those orchestrations to songs like 'Love to Love.' It just wouldn't be the same without all that. Maybe not in sync with today's current scene, but I think it's become a trademark for us. *Lights Out* is my favourite of the three I was on. My girlfriend bought a CD copy of it recently, and I hadn't listened to it for many, many years. The drums are very small and all that, but you have to remember, it was a different time."

As a gentle dig, the band treated Ron like one of their overbearing instructors from school, presenting him with a gown and cap. To smooth over ruffled feathers throughout the sessions, Ron would end the long days by treating the band to dinner.

"I don't know; we recorded it in London," laughs Pete, asked if he can envision a Queen influence to the album. "Funny enough, I think Michael has that tone that Brian May gets, but I wouldn't say that it is so much like Queen. But I think at that time we took a lot of care with our song writing, although I guess we've always taken care with our song writing. Ron Nevison was a big part of putting things together, although having said that, we jammed a lot of the stuff. We'd take certain elements of our songs and we'd play them; we were always open to things. Also, Paul Raymond's keyboards had a lot of special things about them."

Special things, indeed. *Lights Out* is full of them. Finally the band would be rewarded for their years of toil. Fully three tracks on the album, "Too Hot to Handle," "Lights Out" and "Love to Love," would become live highlights, with "Electric Phase" also ranking fondly in fan lists of favourites. Sadly, only one more studio album would be birthed with Schenker at the axe position (before the reunion in the '90s). Interestingly, 1978's *Obsession* would do better business in Britain versus *Lights Out*, where the reverse is true in America—*Lights Out* sold better, with the band fading on the follow-up. The subsequent *Strangers in the Night* double live record from December of '78 is viewed as one of the greatest live albums of all time, with "Lights Out" and "Love to Love" providing particularly heavy emotional heat.

"We did *Lights Out* at Air Studios and the budget didn't matter," recalls Phil wistfully, adding the final word on the assembly of the record. "It was luxurious and fun, the bar open every night. Ronnie used to lose it sometimes: 'Will you get the fuck out of here and take them fuckin' people with you!' We always took awhile to record—or rather, we took a long time getting what Ron wanted (laughs)."

Interestingly, just after the smoke had cleared, Andy expressed a slight tinge of regret as well, concerning the hiring on of Ron. "We decided to make a big change on this album because we weren't happy with the last one. We thought the production lacked a little bit, so we thought we'd find ourselves a good producer. I'm pleased with it with one or two reservations. The biggest problem with having a very good producer is that they always tend to be too strongly minded. They tend to point you in their direction rather than work so much for you. It was okay, but we found the more we were getting into Ron, the more we got into taking his ideas, the stronger he got then, the more he tried to steer you; it was a little bit difficult."

Conversely, "Leo was okay because he was learning to produce, the same as we were learning to work with a producer. Leo spent more time in the studio than we had, so it was not so bad, but then he hadn't had the actual album experience, whereas Ron had a lot of experience doing albums. Basically it was taking too long for us to progress. We felt that the band needed a more 'go ahead' producer. While we were with Leo, we were progressing but very, very slowly."

In the spirit of the punk times, the NME spoke of UFO and *Lights Out* in terms of obsolescence, Bob Edmands writing that the band's style "falls somewhere between Free and Deep Purple: rasping shrieks from vocalist Phil Mogg and aggressive screams from guitarist Michael Schenker. No doubt these guys would like to be right up there with the dinosaurs they emulate, and while it is a funny time for a heavy rock band to be taking off, there's a strong chance they'll make it. Whereas the likes of Bad Company, for example, rock out with the first track on each album and then go weak-kneed afterwards, UFO make almost every track a first track. To anyone who grew up on a diet of Hendrix and Led Zeppelin, it will probably seem tame enough, but compared to many of the more undeserving heirs to their legacy, UFO are classy indeed."

Dependably, Geoff Barton is the man on record for Sounds, following up an extensive article extolling the band's virtues live with this review expressing disappointment. He expresses a warning as well, as he cautions those who just had their faces tore clean off by the band in concert, that the new record is kind of limp.

"*Lights Out* tries hard. Problem is, just as you think the album is about to take off, it flounders—on one side with the balladic 'Try Me,' ponderous and completely out of context, on the other with a depressingly dispensable version of Love's 'Alone Again Or,' just about a carbon copy of the original version, a pretty pointless reworking. Grouped around these two cuts we have the riotous 'Lights Out,' the immaculately constructed 'Love to Love' and the exciting, impression-making 'Another Suicide.' But all lose impetus appreciably once 'Try Me' or 'Alone Again Or' come around. Leo Lyons has vacated the production chair in favour of Ron Nevison, who does a competent if unremarkable job. What would've been really great, however, would have been to have had a hot American producer on the boards—Jack Douglas or Bob Ezrin, maybe even Eddie Kramer—to bring UFO out of their shells."

Touring for *Lights Out* was extensive, including a leg with Rush on that band's *A Farewell to Kings* tour in America, to close out 1977. This was the first leg back for Michael, who returned just in the nick of time after temporarily removing himself from the band for a mental health vacation (more on this later).

Canada's "baby Rush" Max Webster was also on the bill, with the band's bassist Mike Tilka recalling that, "There was a huge fuel crisis in the States, and I remember playing in Tennessee, it was an extremely cold winter, and it was really hard to get gasoline. We're driving in the van and we'd put a piece of cardboard in front of the radiator so the water gets hotter, because we were driving with blankets on our knees. Because the front of the van is just tin. It was freezing! The guys in Rush would sometimes... Kim and Gary would sometimes ride in their bus. We played an arena, and I remember the kids were all wearing jean jackets and stuff and it was freezing. UFO was nuts. Phil Mogg was crazy. I saw them later with Wireless; there's even more stories. The guitar player, Michael Schenker, he practiced all the time. He never talked. He didn't socialize with us in the band. In rehearsal, you could hear him practice; if you're at a gig, you would see him practice; the guy was scary. Pete Way? Yeah, he was drunk all the time. He used to fall over—on stage."

Max Webster's leader Kim Mitchell also has fond memories of standing with the Rush guys and watching Michael sound check, mouths agape. Into the early '80s, rumours flew of Michael perhaps putting together some sort of project band with Geddy Lee and Neil Peart.

"UFO were funny," recalls Rush guitarist Alex Lifeson on life on the road with UFO. "We did a show with them, and I remember it was in Spokane (laughs). It's amazing that I remember these places. I just remember looking over and they were all standing there in these robes. But they just got these granny robes and they had the big fluffy slippers, and they were really taking the piss out of us." The band was in fact mocking the matching flashy "wizard"-style robes Rush had briefly worn on tour, Pete at times augmenting the story by saying UFO had also put a Mickey Mouse drum kit in front of Neil's for the occasion. Phil mused years later, "We opened for Rush when we first started touring. Vaudeville. That's when Rush were wearing the dressing gowns and the fluffy slippers."

"Man, those dates... ugh, I don't know how we survived them," continues Alex. "Just the level of drinking! Every night with them was a riot, but it was just like heavy, heavy drinking. Those guys would start drinking... they'd show up for sound check but they never did a sound check. They'd show up for sound check so they could start drinking, you know, because they knew the booze was at the gig and it was free. We'd always see them before we went on. They would go back to their dressing room, change, and always come up to our dressing room before we went on. They were tanked by that time! But they were just kind of fun drunks. Pete Way especially; he was just so hilarious the whole time."

"I still remember they let us take our bus into their neighbourhood," recalls Phil (in a notorious interview with the author that was so incomprehensible at times—but always hilarious—that the label representative called back later to apologize and offer another chat with Mogg at a later time). "I don't know whether it was Geddy's house or... they said, 'No no, it'll be fine. Park your bus.' I remember Pete going through his record collection and pulling out albums and going, 'What's this album here?!' Genesis, or something ridiculous. But I remember them being really nice."

"And we also played one of their songs through our dressing room to theirs, which was... hang on, what was it? One of their ridiculous songs, or sorry, one of their songs (laughs). Alex came back... oh, I know what it is: 'I have dined on honeydew' (sings it real high). So we was thinking we were smart, and Alex, the guitarist, came back with 'Rock Bottom,' through the glass, through the door. But no, we had a great time with them. They were a great band to play with, with Brooksy and Lurch, and the slippers. I remember all that stuff—wow. Because they were wearing them long outfits and nightgowns. I don't know what Canadians do, but very sort of brutal English, it's 'Oi, what you fackers doing?!' Kind of a bit crude would be the word. We nailed the slippers to the floor, so they couldn't be removed. But, they came back with... as good as we gave, they came back with more. So I think the dice were thrown even there. Hey, anyone who allows their bus to be driven to their front door, and allows them into your home, with a load of groupies on, and lets them into your home—and that was Geddy—I think that's good; that's pretty bold. So, no, I think he stood up very well there. I'm talking about really raw groupies, and to allow that, 'Yeah, that's okay,' I think they're cool guys."

"I personally had nothing to do with the rest of the guys," says Michael, on the rest of his band's intoxicating, intoxicated and toxic presence, once UFO hit the road. "I had my own schedule and I was doing things my own way as a musician, which meant that every time we would get to the next concert, before I even go to the hotel, they would drop me off at the concert hall. I would take my case with me—or whatever, wash bag—and freshen up at the concert. But first I started to practice for a few hours. I did that every day. They would drop me off at the concert place, and I would practice, until they came. Then we would do sound check, and I would carry on practicing, and then we would play. And then after we usually would get pretty high. I don't really watch other people. I kind of prefer to live and let live, and so I don't really hang around what other people are doing. That doesn't really interest me either. I just know what I was doing, which I just explained."

But the *Lights Out* tour, with all of the record's success, and the growing buzz on the band, turned out to be too much for Michael, who suddenly went AWOL, replaced by Paul Chapman in the states, for the above amusing interactions with Rush. Fortunately for the band, Michael was found and cajoled back in time for the writing and recording of the next record.

"The funny thing is, I don't focus on commercial success," said Michael, by way of explanation. "The thing I focus on was to become a great guitarist. My focus was never to be famous or to be successful or to be rich or anything. Other than, I wanted to be able to create goose pimples. Because that's what happened to me when those people like Jeff Beck and Leslie West and those guys, that's what made it for me. I want people to do that too. By making that decision, that was when I started to just focus on being a great guitarist, just like those guys. Actually having that success there with *Lights Out*, in fact, I was running away from it. I was like wait a minute! What's going on here? It was too much. So I was actually scared of success. Because I never focused on it. I always focused on what I really loved doing, which was being a guitar player, that aspect itself, the leads, the details of those emotions that go through all different areas and all sorts of extremes, from loud to quiet, from heavy to romantic, all emotional aspects as possible—they're all a reflection of myself. That's what I was interested in, and at some point much later success became the icing on the cake, but it was never really a necessity for me."

"I left because I was afraid of touring," continues Schenker. "People thought I was God and I couldn't handle it. I mean, people were walking around outside the arenas or whatever with banners in their hands, holding it up, written on it 'Schenker is God.' I was very fragile when I was young, and very shy. It was kind of scary at times. When I was starting out in music, I wasn't really thinking too much about how rich or famous I was going to be. When it gets too good, I'm saying bye-bye (laughs). To me, it was just music. Music was the priority; the music and I were one. People could easily take advantage of me. Because I was so into the music, they would come up for the right time for them, to have me sign stupid stuff. I would be in a mess. But they would take advantage of my focus, you know what I mean? They would come up and say, 'Hey Michael, quickly, sign this, otherwise we can't carry on this recording' or whatever. They would kind of intimidate me. I would sign it, not understanding how bad of a move it could have been. So I had a few things created because of that that weren't good for me, you know? But that's part of life, I guess, and it's in the past."

"But yes, the first time I left in '77, was because *Lights Out* became a hit in America, and all I saw in front of me was endless touring, and I didn't want to do that. It was the pressure of touring and being wanted more than I would want to be wanted. I also knew that if I tried to explain that to them, they would just talk me into it. So I just had to go. I sold everything and went with my girlfriend to the south of France, bought a couple of mopeds and then drove to where I used to go camping with my parents, between Barcelona and Tarragona in Spain. Stayed there for awhile, went back to Germany via Munich, found an apartment there, moved straight in the same day we arrived. Then from there on, I wanted to know where my equipment was. I got Pete on the phone, and he persuaded me to come back. I had some rest, and I guess I was ready to continue, and that was it."

"I don't know what drives Michael," laughs Phil, remembering the incident. "But touring absolutely knackers people and he was young and got a lot of attention. Then again, it's what he wanted. We didn't ask where he'd been, but he bought a moped, drove to Dover and went to Spain, then got a tent and camped out on Clapham Common. He did this the same way to the Scorpions, though, so he's reliable! (laughs). He went. Fuck 'im. That was it."

Press at the time had Michael joining the Moonies, a popular and scary cult at the time, run with an iron fist by Reverend Sun Myung Moon. Counters Michael, "Yes, there were all sorts of stories; that was one of Phil Mogg's clever little tricks. He was just kind of giving the people some interesting stories to keep the whole thing going or something. I didn't tell anybody where I went. That's why it was so mysterious. Not even my mom, I told. Because I knew that they would try to find out. I just wanted away from everything."

As Phil explained to Scene magazine, "We had three weeks off before the American tour, and we had a tape for the BBC to mix down. I phoned him up and asked if he was coming down. He said yeah, and never showed up, which is very unusual for him to do. I asked Andy to stop by his place and check things out, because he'd had troubles with drinking in the past; he's been in the hospital a couple of times because of it. Anyway, there was nobody there. His landlady said he'd gone, moved, and didn't say where he was going. We sent someone to check with his brother and family in Germany, checked his friends and haunts in London—not a trace. He used to get this religious material from San Francisco when he was living with me. Purification of the soul and all that crap. I know he takes it seriously. He may have joined up with one of them. We always called him Jeckyll and Hyde; usually it was Jeckyll until the old firewater got in him. Anything's possible."

So Paul Chapman was bounced into service again, albeit briefly. "It's a difficult post to fill," reflected Mogg, "because we are essentially a lead guitar band; most of the playing complements the leads. But Paul had just finished recording, and we asked him if he wanted the spot for this tour. He accepted and we went straight into rehearsals. The first three gigs we've done we've had people yelling, 'Where's Schenker?' I mean, it's an obvious thing, but it's disappeared after a couple of numbers. They'd have a right to be pissed-off if we gave them just a substitute, but if you lay another hot guitarist on them, they wait to see what he can do, and Paul's a very hot guitarist. We're generating more energy on stage now, I think. He plays in a similar style to Michael but more raw and aggressive, generating more excitement."

Indeed manager Wilf Wright (who, incidentally, had also managed Robin Trower, another Chrysalis act) had stated, "Because of Schenker's involvement and fascination with mysticism and religion, he may have joined the Moonies." But after Michael had been stopped in Munich for speeding on his motorbike, and actually recognized by the policeman, Wilf now was saying, "Schenker, who was suffering from nervous exhaustion following that long and taxing European tour, could not face the thought of the extensive tour which the band had set up for July and August, and therefore decided to take it upon himself to 'go missing.'"

"Oh, I've been stalked all right, big time," says Michael in closing, asked how bad the pressure had gotten. "Conned and everything. For 12 years I was stalked. I have been conned and stalked, and tricked etc. etc., and a few times, and pretty heavily too. I didn't know it was illegal for people to do that, so I could've pulled the plug on that. But I didn't. So I was cleverly manipulated and intimidated and trapped into a particular space. When I watched the movie *Matchstick Men*, it kind of hit me; it gave me a little bit of insight into what happened."

Chapter Eight
Obsession

"How come I'm the one without any balls?"

Touring hard, flying high and bickering loud on the heels of their successful *Lights Out* album of 1977, UFO commenced work on a record that would be oddly cold, dry and heavy, harkening back to the harsh environs of *Force It*, although packed with more detailed songs chopped and presented as the band's most event-packed album to date. Yet even though the shorter and numerous songs made for a more immediate and active listen, the recurring theme was a live sort of heaviness amidst the uneasy feeling that there were less hooks to be found compared to the record's predecessor.

But first the odd album cover, one of the more distinctive offerings from famed British art house Hipgnosis. "I remember Michael saying, 'Why am I the one without the balls in the eyes?'" recalls Pete Way. "With Hipgnosis, you sort of put yourself in their hands and you held your breath to see what they were going to come up with. That's me and Phil on the front, and Andy and Paul on the back. We didn't physically have balls to put in our eyes. That was done in the art room." Vocalist Phil Mogg, of course, recalls the conversation more like Michael saying, "How come I'm the one without any balls?"

Schenker good-naturedly concurs. "I was always suspicious about the cover art (laughs). I mean, it was really weird, going to the photo session. It was like, why are they all going to have bubbles in their eyes and not me? I was wondering, what on earth are these guys up to? Why are they all having a suit and tie on and I'm having this scruffy old shirt? What is the meaning? I guess, they never really explained it to me. guess maybe my English wasn't good enough to understand anyway."

Wrote David Fricke from Circus, describing the *Obsession* cover art, "Against the cold blue backdrop of the animal surgery lab at UCLA are pictured the faces of Mogg, Way, Raymond and Parker—dark hair slicked black with ball bearings covering eyes, nose, mouth and ears. The blond, sullen, German-speaking Schenker stands background centre, looking very much like the mute mystery man who walked off last year without a trace on the eve of UFO's US tour and returned three months later with no explanations."

Continues Fricke, "Peter Christopherson of Hipgnosis, the British firm which designed this and all other UFO covers, claims the idea for the design had been on the drawing board for months and that 'it was decided to use Michael as the odd man in the shot even before he disappeared. The combination of title and picture was just a happy accident.'" Mogg told Fricke, with a proverbial wink, that it was all just "a good laugh and good art. But then it's always good to keep the cover as a separate piece of art. That way if the album isn't any good, we can sell the cover."

When I asked Aubrey Powell at Hipgnosis, about the general vibe of the aggregate of Hipgnosis covers, myself warily venturing a few adjectives, Powell, to my relief said, "I would agree with the words you just used. Edgy, sterile, precise. One of the key secrets to Hipgnosis was, if you look at it carefully, is that everything was sharp focus front to back. Which is not how the eye sees it. It's impossible. You can paint like that, but you can't do photography like that. What we did was create collages. For example—and I know we talked about this for *Force It*—on *Houses of the Holy*, this is a very good example, where everything in the foreground is crystal sharp. Again, with things like UFO or... let's take Styx as an example, *Pieces of Eight*. That cover, we've got a bunch of women on Easter Island, wearing Easter Island earrings, and they're all looking like, let's say, the daughters of the American Revolution, kind of characters. Very conservative women, very sterile, and then in the background, they're on Easter Island, and that's all a collage all put together. If you look at it, everything is crystal sharp from the earring in the foreground to the Easter Island figures in the back."

"That's not how the eye sees things," continues Powell. "It's a deliberate sort of, I suppose, almost pop art in a way; you know how pop art sees things. You can paint like that, you can do cartoons like that, and we followed that sort of way of doing things. The same goes for *Never Say Die*—the pilots are sharp, the planes are sharp, the sky is sharp. It's not like a real photograph. That was one of the things we looked for. So edginess, sure, plus I wanted to create things that were eye-catching, that were unusual, that people had to think about the cover. I wanted people to think about the cover, not just accept what was there. 'Oh, that's a pretty picture.' Think about what it meant, what had gone into it, what interpretation did you want to put on it. We were definitely looking for that."

As for *Obsession*, and Michael's lack of balls, "That's absolutely true," laughs Aubrey. "That's a true story. That cover, I shot that in California at the Veterans Hospital in LA. Again, it's a collage, so if you look at it, everything is sharp front to back. It's an impossible kind of image. But you're absolutely right, and that's true that he said that to Phil Mogg: 'How come I'm the guy without balls?' They were ruthless. I mean, there were some bands I worked with that had a very funny sense of humour. I still know Phil Mogg to this day. He's a very, very funny man. He's a survivor. They were ruthless in their sense of humour, and they would take the piss out of Schenker something terrible. Although he was a most brilliant guitarist, he had a lot of problems with that. It created a lot of problems. Tension within the band. But, you know, Phil Mogg was there, and Pete Way too, they were never going to give up on that kind of activity. They're too English and he's still doing it. They're still doing tours of Japan and North America. We share the same hairdresser—that's why I know all this."

Past the wrapper and into the record, Phil figures that, "*Lights Out*, our first one with Nevison, that was a bit of an eye-opener. That was great, because of his experience. He also got us our first hit record as such, in terms of charting. And *Obsession*, I mainly remember it being humourous. I think we did that one when we was living in LA. I seem to recall it being more of a fun album; funny things happened. It was odd to start recording in a post office, with the mobile; and just the whole atmosphere of the thing was quite amusing. Oh, and I think Hipgnosis came over to do the cover, which they shot in the veterinary wing of UCLA; just odd things like that, kind of getting dressed up for that. Michael's saying things like, 'Oh, what is this cover?'"

"I had a penchant for recording in odd places," explains Nevison.

"Not odd places, but with the remote truck. I built one for Ronnie Lane; I did Zeppelin with that particular truck, in a house that they had rented and in LA I carried on. I did the first Babys album *Broken Heart*, which was after the *Lights Out* album, with the Record Plant remote truck, at a house out near Lake Sherwood out in Westlake Village. I just like that kind of thing. I did the first Bad Company albums in houses. One of them in Hampshire, one of them out in Clearwell Castle in Wales and one at this big mansion in the south of France. So I like that sort of thing."

"I don't remember what initially brought me into that, but I think that the Record Plant had a fire in studio C, which, was the room I liked to cut rock 'n' roll drums in. I asked them to start looking around for a replacement, and I would use the truck. They couldn't find anything, except they found this vacant postal annex, this sorting centre, in Beverly Hills, like one big huge room. It had a couple of bathrooms, everything we needed, for us to set up our stuff. A cordoned-off little area. Except for the fact it was near a hotel and these people complained... I used to have a camera set up in the truck, closed circuit, and I remember seeing policemen listening to Schenker while he was playing, like to stop playing (laughs). I mean, they were nice about it, but they had a complaint from the hotel, L'Ermitage, which was a really nice hotel. It was like ten o'clock at night. So we agreed not to go past nine or something like that, with all the racket. It all worked out in the end."

"I like the 'liveness' of big rooms," continues Ron, "and I wanted UFO to have a different sound for this particular record. I will never forget Schenker, right in the middle of this hall, right next to his Marshall amp, I am watching him from the truck on closed circuit TV. Like I say, he is playing and two policemen come in and tap him on the shoulder and he almost had a heart attack. I went out there and said that we would shut it down. I told them not to worry about it. We told them we would not work this late again. I will never forget the look on Michael's face!"

As for the value of a Michael Schenker within UFO, Ron figures, "It's not just his playing, it's his writing. He is really responsible for most of the really good stuff in UFO. They all contributed. Pete Way contributed, but Michael did the majority of the writing of these great anthems that they did. Schenker was the man, no question about it. I love the guitar work on *Obsession*. I did more parts with Michael, different licks in-between phrases... I did tons of stuff, much more than on *Lights Out*."

"We got a good overdub sound," said Phil, speaking with Beat Instrumental at the time. "It was very wooden, which made it sound very live." Added Pete, "That was the thing—we wanted the album to sound live, because we feel quite often that the best sounds for this band is just that, so that's what we worked towards. You see, basically we're the sort of band whose albums get knocked in music paper reviews—it's easy for them to knock the albums—but when it comes to watching us at gigs, they'll knock the gigs and afterwards they'll say, 'But the people liked it.' Know what I mean?"

The postal building—West 3rd Carrier Station in Beverly Hills—was only one site used. The band also recorded at C.P. McGregors at Wilshire and Western, which was later purchased by Stevie Wonder and renamed Wonderland. Nevison, Mike Clink and the boys also made use of the Record Plant Mobile.

Once inside the final product, one was greeted instantly with the record's emotional anchor, lead single "Only You Can Rock Me" rumbling and trundling forth, blessed with a richness of melody that took the track into the regal realm of heavy Queen. It is a favourite of Pete's, one of three co-credits for him on the record. "Yeah, the guitar riff was a riff of mine. It was quite a simple thing, sort of Rolling Stones-like. Paul Raymond kind of added the icing to the cake. That keyboard sound, that organ, is very important. It's a very good balance. It's catchy without being poppy and it's rock without being really heavy."

"That was something Pete came up with," affirms Michael, "which was a Status Quo, blues, Rolling Stones type of thing. That's basically what he's good at. Again, there was something missing melodically. I guess maybe the combination between his Stones type of approach and my melodic approach combined, always made the songs interesting, because it could have two different aspects to it."

That's a key point right there, whether Michael fully gets it or not. Pete could write dependable "Louie Louie" chord progressions all day and night, but spice it up with a little taste of the Teutonic, a little sense of the upper crust, and an exotic alloy is created that few could conjure, save, again, for Thin Lizzy, who could also write in these two directions and then snap the parts together.

Phil, who turns in a "Boys Are Back in Town"-type salvo lyrically, sums up the track this way. "That was a straight Pete riff, the main verse, and then Michael added the part where he makes it that little bit different, maybe the breakdown into the solo, which was a good collaboration between the three of us, really. That worked really well with the three of us working together."

The boomy feel of the album from the sonic spectrum end of things would set *Obsession* apart within the catalogue. This can be heard most clearly on "Pack It Up," which Way describes as "us being a little bit Led Zeppelin-ish, because we like that type of thing and it's not difficult for us to play in that style." Indeed, the song "recoils" much like "Immigrant Song," and Phil ever so slightly adopts Plant's vocal phrasings as well as some of his melody choices.

Michael offers this reminiscence of the track. "'Pack It Up'... Phil Mogg, for some reason, he didn't want to know about it (laughs); I don't know why. I remember doing that in the rehearsal studio, a big rehearsal studio in Los Angeles, and I remember Andy and Phil had an argument or something and that riff came up. I think it wasn't suitable for Phil somehow; he couldn't get a grasp on it and he just kind of went away and we carried on ourselves and we arranged it and got to the point where we just put it on the side. When Ron Nevison heard it, he wanted that song, so Phil had to work with it. He actually did something good with it."

"Mainly because I probably couldn't get any vocals to go with it," counters Phil, when asked to answer to Michael's remarks that he didn't take to the song too kindly. "I didn't overly dislike it. Sometimes Michael might have had the impression that if I was having difficulty with a song... and I think I was having difficulty with that one, getting something I was happy with. I tend to get a bit grumpy if I can't come up with something I'm happy with, you see. So he probably, you know... in his German way (laughs)."

The sonic terrain of the album was achieved partly through its novel recording environment, partly through the vision of big-spending producer Ron Nevison, brought back by a recalcitrant Chrysalis after the success of *Lights Out*. "We recorded a lot of with the Record Plant Mobile in LA," explains Pete, giving his side of the story. "We used a huge post office actually, a big old building. And then we finished it off at the Record Plant. That was quite adventurous to actually use a mobile. But I think Ron Nevison had done that with the first Bad Company album. It was something that we thought perhaps would give the album a bit more of a raw edge; plus you could always put the polish on it in the studio. Ron was great. You can learn an awful lot from working with Ron, very talented. You felt very comfortable putting yourself into Ron's hands. Basically he teaches you a lot, but at the same time he works with you because he thinks you're good at what you do. If he likes what you do, he lets you do what you want but at the same time he's very meticulous. He gets the best out of you. It took about three months I think. I can't remember how long exactly, because you start work on it yourself, writing, and then you are rehearsing—three or four months I suppose."

"I like the album," figures Schenker, offering his two cents, "kind of better than *Lights Out* in a way. Even though *Lights Out* was a more controlled album, *Obsession* was more of a rocking album because it was kind of done in an old post office and we wanted a big room sound. We wanted it to have something like a John Bonham drum sound. For me it was a great album. Some people prefer it, some people don't, compared to *Lights Out*. People either love *Obsession* or hate it. *Lights Out* is more of a studio album and *Obsession* sounds more live. Because not everyone is attracted to live sounds, like when you get the room sound; that's what I mean by live. It wasn't done in a live performance, but it was done in a post office, a big, big room, a large building which had a lot of ambience. But some people like a more direct sound. So *Lights Out* is more direct, close-mic'ed, and *Obsession* has more ambience. The songs, to me, there's not that much difference. I like both albums. I've always liked a bit more of a live sound because I've always been a John Bonham fan."

"But being not that much of a technical person, I didn't know that the more live sound you put on the tape, the other things are going to suffer," adds Schenker. "If you're just a musician who dreams about sound, you can screw things up very easily. If you're a specialist on sounds, if you're a sound engineer, you know what you can use and what you should not use too much of, in order to keep everything in perspective. It's difficult for the musician. You have a lot of dreams when you are the musician and you have a lot of ideas, and you would love to see them then put into reality, but sometimes it cannot be done, due to technical problems."

Perhaps the twinned or comparable piece to "Pack It Up" is "Hot 'n' Ready," another panoramic, wide-angled, canyon-like metal rocker, arguably the heaviest song on the album. Remarks Pete, "In those days we kind of worked things through more than coming in with the complete thing. The same with my things. Because we played together so much through touring, we had this thing where we quite instinctively were able to follow somebody's idea. The actual rhythm pattern of that one is sort of the hook on its own. I don't know if that's the right term. It's not a pop hook. But it kind of grabs you."

What also grabs is the number of hot licks riddled throughout "Hot 'n' Ready," culminating in what is arguably the record's best guitar solo. Yet at that point Michael isn't done, creating an understated but inspiring dialogue with himself to fade out the track. Phil's lyric flashes like the muzzle of a gun as well, opening with the hot-clockin' line, "You knock me out, you're like a well-oiled Smith & Wesson."

"It all comes down to being yourself," reflects Michael, on the art of soloing. "Anyone can do that, but most people have a problem doing that. To be yourself, and to be okay with that, is where you create originality. You can enjoy it very much rather than being in the rat race and competing with people. Art is not a competition. It is just an expression and it is who you are. Most people can do that, but most people just don't choose to do so. Most people want to be part of a trend and they want to get a piece of the pie and that is why that world is a bit confusing. If you have as much fun as I have, just creating, then you have already reaped all of the rewards. That, in itself, is amazing and the rest is all by-products."

"Being yourself is endless," continues Michael. "Expression is endless. The key is to actually know that and to do it. If a person is, you know, copying or being part of a trend and being part of the rat race, then it puts pressure on you and you don't have very much freedom to create anything. Real creation is where you're not part of the rat race and you just simply, you know, have fun putting notes together and enjoying the outcome of it. For each individual, when people do that, then they express their own colour, which they only can express. I cannot express your colour, or your colours. The moment you know that is when you start enjoying who you are, then everything else is a by-product. Everything happens the way you want it to happen. Each person has their own way of finding. Once a person makes the decision of self-expression they automatically develop their own way of doing things."

"Basically, it is what I have done since I was 18. I stopped copying others and I stopped listening to music. I stop consuming, because consuming puts a groove in your head that you cannot get away from, especially if you do it for many years. Basically, I play and discover on a regular basis, and when I bump into something I really like, like a five-second piece of something, when it is time to make a record, I put my pieces together—that is what I do."

Moving on, UFO's pure pop sensibility is represented by side two's second track and "Only You Can Rock Me" B-side "Cherry," which was flirted with by some stations at the time as a possible hit, accompanying "Cherry Baby" by Starz, "Cherry Bomb" by The Runaways and "Cherry Oh Baby" by the Rolling Stones as songs looking to cash in on the cherry craze of the day, all of those issued in 1977 except for the Runaways medium hit, which came out in 1976. This was another track that started with Pete Way, who figures in the writing credits more than is usual with UFO, Pete chalking it up to Nevison liking his ideas.

"That was kind of interesting because I had this bass riff and Phil said, 'You know, I can sing to that' and we built on it. It was built very much around that bass guitar and there was a catchiness there. It's a rock 'n' roll song with a twist. It's unusual to have a bass guitar riff start it off." Phil's lyric for "Cherry" is colourful enough, depicting a band passing through town and the nomadic rocker stricken by a table dancer who has more charm going on than her circumstance would let on. Continues Pete, "Yeah, 'Cherry' was always a very popular song and I'm not just saying that because I co-wrote it with Phil. But it's about us being in Austin, Texas, and going to a dance place on a day off, and the girl is called Cherry, and well, I didn't like the words, actually; I might've helped. So it's a little bit different. But yes, inspirational young lady; very inspirational, I can assure you."

Pete's garage rock chord progression combines ably and sympathetically with Phil's memorable "I feel just like a rolling stone" line, which he belts out with conviction. There's no doubt Pete would have made an excellent bassist for the Stones, at least in photographs, be they on stage, out on the town or out on bail.

"Lookin' Out for No. 1" is another odd moment on the album, a respite of sorts. "I think that was like Ron's masterpiece there," muses Pete. "It has real strings in it. We were saying how we had never done an album with an orchestra, but actually we had, because all of Ron's stuff was with live strings." Phil's lyric, not one of his stronger ones (in fact, this whole album is comparatively weak in that department), revisits terrain that snapshots the concept of boy turning to man, more energy than brains.

All in all, *Obsession* kept returning to the rock in concentric circles, the slow, menacing trudge of "Ain't No Baby," the funk of "You Don't Fool Me" and the hard Foreigner of "One More for the Rodeo" all adding to the metal end of the record. Of note, Michael is pretty sure that "One More for the Rodeo" is "a Paul Raymond song," going on to add that "Paul was never really credited with the songs in those days because he was owing money to other people so they paid the money to Phil or somebody and they took the credit and gave the money to Paul. I don't know how it worked; there was something like that going on. But Paul Raymond actually deserves much more credit than he got, because he wrote some of the better songs when he joined the band for *Lights Out* and *Obsession* and so on. I don't remember which songs, but there are a few of them."

Paul himself, unsurprisingly, is helpful in that regard. "There were quite a few that I wasn't credited for on *Obsession*. Pete, actually, he's credited for quite a lot that I did. 'I Ain't No Baby,' 'One More for the Rodeo,' 'Lookin' Out for No. 1;' these are all songs I wrote with Phil. Favourites of the ones I've done? I haven't done that many. I think 'Just Another Suicide' (from *Lights Out*) is a good song. 'I Ain't No Baby,' 'One More for the Rodeo,' 'Lookin' Out for No. 1.' (*No Place o Run*'s) 'Take It or Leave It?' Nah, you can take it or leave it, that one (laughs). That's it; there's not that many songs of mine on there."

At the *Obsession* stage of the game, Paul's gear consisted of a 1967 Les Paul Junior (played upside down as he has indicated), and for keyboard equipment, a discontinued Hammond M102 powered by a 760 Leslie cabinet, a Mini-Moog, a Yamaha electric grand, a Solina string machine and some Moog Taurus pedals. For amplification, Paul was using a couple of Fender Dual Showmans. As for the rest of the guys, Michael had his Gibson Flying V, Andy pounded on white Ludwigs with two bass drums and Pete worked his way through three different basses, a Precision, a Thunderbird and a Gibson.

"One More for the Rodeo" houses, arguably, Phil's best lyric of the record, Phil in succinct film noire fashion tsk-tsking over another dreamer turned corpse, another pretender felled by too much aspiration for infamy in the danger zone.

"Blues licks," says Paul, when asked about his main inspiration or influence when writing. "I've always had me feet in the blues, because of coming from that background, Chicken Shack, and then into Savoy Brown, surrounded by the British blues thing. So I had a lot of blues riffs hanging around for a long time, and we showed them to Phil, because Phil has an amazing knack of making something out of nothing, just a simple thing. He'd sing something, and you would go, 'How did he think of that? That's really clever.' So it's just kind of stuff from the blues days, I guess."

And the reason this non-crediting happened? "Bad publishing deal, previous management, with Savoy Brown. Looking back now, it would probably have been better to take the credit and not be paid. Because it's always better to take the credit, because it lives on forever. So they say, 'You wrote that song.' That was a managerial mistake, something for which I've never spoken to the manager again. But anyway, that's a personal issue."

"Well, they're both heavily orchestrated, aren't they?" queries Paul, with respect to *Lights Out* and *Obsession*. "We tried for a bigger drum sound on *Obsession*. There's a lot of echo on the guitars (laughs). I listened to that record not long ago and I thought God, there's so much there... we used the kitchen sink on it (laughs). There's also natural ambience from the room on *Obsession*; it's very much an album of its time, I suppose. That's what somebody described it as. But still, considering that we were doing tour/album, tour/album, and we came straight off the road and we had to make that record, there's some good stuff on there, like 'Only You Can Rock Me,' things that have become mainstays of the set."

Michael had the following to say, with respect to a couple of very light moments on the record. "'Arbory Hill' was something I did on my flute. That was written in England. I was doing this thing on my flute and I remember my girlfriend coming home from work and wanting to go to bed. I said, annoyed, 'Just give me a minute, give me a moment!' I was still working on it and I almost had it. I'd never really worked a flute before so I got really into it and I remember that day, I'm smashing my guitar, because I was almost completing that song and my girlfriend was nagging and nagging me. If you're in an extremely creative mode, and you get nagged on that level, you kind of get short-tempered. So that's what I remember. It's an interesting contrast. I'm working on a very beautiful soft song but something drastic happens. So I had the experience finding out, when you break your guitar, when you're smashing it up, that when people put it back together, it plays better than when you buy it new. It becomes custom-made."

Michael says the inspiration to take up the "flute" (in other interviews, he calls this a recorder) and add that into "Arbory Hill" came from hearing John Paul Jones play recorders on "Stairway to Heaven."

"'Born to Lose' is something I did as well," continues Michael. "I did an instrumental thing and we put vocals around it. Most of the slow, beautiful songs that we did, they usually started off as an instrumental and then I would give the tape to Phil with all these different things and he would go, 'Oh, I would like to sing to this song' and so on. Then we would just kind of take some parts out of the instrumental that were more suitable for vocals, and then just make a song out of it."

Pete reflects on the pressures at this particular point in the chemical-fuelled UFO saga. "I thought the band were progressing all the time. We definitely had our own sound. Like with the *Strangers in the Night* thing, it sort of led on from that. It was the band probably at their best for a while. We'd done all the touring and we kind of got used to working with Ron; it was a high point. It's difficult to say how we were getting along, because Michael did leave shortly after that. I don't know how Michael's spirituality entered into the equation. I think Michael was more into the spirituality of the bottle at that point. No, I'm joking. But Michael has always been interested in the spiritual side. He certainly didn't push it on anybody."

"As a band, we were again at one of those points where we were having to play, and having to go into the studio. It probably let out a lot of energy into the record but perhaps we could have done with a break. Because we went straight back on the road and did *Strangers*. But Ron was always so hands-on. I was never shocked by anything he brought in. He worked so hard on it, so hard that it was like his life depended on it. He gave it his all and he demanded that all his bands played really well, which makes for better records. And that's not always the case. But we respected Ron so much. When he was sort of cracking the whip or getting really angry, it was because he was passionate for it."

"Ron had a different style," adds Phil on the subject. "I think he did a great job on *Obsession*. It was Ron and Mike Clink as the engineer, who went on to produce Guns N' Roses, which I found out later. We had a good combination there."

Melody Maker's review of *Obsession* read, in part, as follows: "One thing is certain—UFO have created for themselves a genuine hard rock anthem with 'Only You Can Rock Me,' the opening track that has a memorably simple melody line, and is doubtless an immediate audience fave. It is followed immediately by 'Pack It Up (and Go),' which is totally surrogate Zeppelin (something to do with producer Ron Nevison? Check him out on your Zeppelin sleeves) with sledgehammer drums that almost oust John Bonham from the skin-thrashers' lobotomy stakes, and savage, darting guitar from Schenker, who comes up straight afterwards with acoustic guitar and flute on 'Arbory Hill,' just to prove he can do it without 1000 watts. What UFO do isn't new, but the measured thrust of Schenker's guitar, picking harmonies and runs to mirror and pace Mogg's archetypal hard rock vocals are sufficient to ensure that they do it with enough individuality to keep them in halls full of fans on both sides of the pond."

Public perception was that *Obsession* marked a pronounced drop from the commercial success of *Lights Out*. "I think it was somewhere around the Top 30 (note: No.26 in the UK, No.41 in the US)," recalls Pete. "*Obsession* and *Lights Out* both did pretty good, actually. I think when Michael had gone, we dropped a bit. It's funny, because around that time, we were drawing more and more people to our live concerts. None of our albums actually had hit singles with them. So a lot of our albums continued to sell, rather than have quick sales and then a quick drop-off. They were sort of constantly bought."

Speaking with the NME, Phil boldly stated that the band was about to finally make it with *Obsession*, adding that with UFO, "It's the difference between Aerosmith and Black Sabbath. I'd say we're more contemporary. I'd say we're more contemporary for this year and next year than Led Zeppelin. I feel that we're more current. We're more happening now. Zeppelin was then, and they've remained in that period. They haven't moved. We've moved. We've moved each year and each album. That's it."

Curiously, *Lights Out* reached only No.54 in the UK, but No.23 in the US, meaning that *Lights Out* did better in the states, but *Obsession* triumphed in Britain. By comparison, the double live *Strangers in the Night* would be an even bigger British smash at No.8, while only reaching No.42 in the states. *Obsession* coughed up three singles, "Only You Can Rock Me," "Born to Lose" and "Cherry" (Canada only), but nothing made much of a dent, unless "Only You Can Rock Me" getting to No.50 in the UK can be considered much of a success. Three decades later, the 2008 reissue of the album was under whelming in terms of rarities, offering up only three live versions of songs from the album, suggesting that the vaults were empty, and that every idea had been put to use on the record.

Finally I asked Pete to offer his thoughts on why this particular version of UFO have, since then, so capably entered the lexicon of classic rock. "I'd say it's because our songs were quite commercial in a way, but rock. I think that was one of the keys to the band. We didn't sell out, but we managed to do songs that were still appreciated for the music and the melodies as much as they were for the hard, grinding guitars."

Amen. *Obsession* may not be the UFO album a great many fans point to as a favourite, but at least it demonstrated a brave versatility and will to greatness practiced by more successful '70s behemoths like Sabbath, Purple, Zeppelin and Queen. It is for this reason the band's history is methodically being revised upward, within an increasingly favourable light, UFO and Thin Lizzy alone (you can maybe add co-headlining *Obsession* tour mates Judas Priest to that list) occupying a revered second tier within the British rock aristocracy as it existed in the 1970s.

Chapter Nine
Strangers in the Night

"You start to earn enough money to buy as much coke as you want"

On through the night, like a circus troupe with a bad case of the shakes, UFO goes. They aren't a small band or an unknown band, but they aren't growing in stature either. Less fun, they must look on from the sidelines as AC/DC, Rush, Styx, Kansas, Scorpions and soon Judas Priest pass them by. But at the turn of the decade, UFO notch a milestone of sorts, issuing a double live album that captures the lurching, knuckle-clenched ride sideways quite fetchingly, sparks flying. That record, *Strangers in the Night*, has been the fortuitous recipient of an effect that is like the rewriting of history, but something perhaps more similar to the shaping, simplifying, habitualising and ossifying of history. This has to do with all of us in the press, when asked, plumping off the top of our heads for this particularly sprightly-looking album as one of the greatest live albums of all time.

In case one is wondering, others invariably mentioned in this discussion (when asker and answerer assume a hard rock context, and are at least of a certain advanced vintage) include Kiss – *Alive!*, Thin Lizzy – *Live and Dangerous*, Blue Öyster Cult – *On Your Feet or on Your Knees*, Judas Priest – *Unleashed in the East*, Rush – *All the World's a Stage* and perhaps Iron Maiden's *Live after Death*. Further down the food chain, folks lined up as well for the likes of Foghat – *Live* and Pat Travers – *Go for What You Know*. Additionally, the band were there to witness all too graphically the stratospheric rise of Peter

Frampton through the smash success of his double live album *Frampton Comes Alive!*

UFO's double slab is no more special than any of the above, except for the arguable fact that the difference in increased power from the band's originals to the live renditions represents the biggest gulf or gulp, save for Kiss and maybe the BÖC. Truth be told, the comparatives are all close, but no question, UFO's collections of anthems, once those songs got to *Strangers*, bulged and magnified in power ten-fold.

I find it amusing how a record like this takes on a life of its own. Indeed, granted, the album was "toured," yet still it's funny how years after into the '00s, one hears the boys talk about their live sets, and how they're playing most of the things from *Strangers in the Night*, as if it's just a damn good studio album of the band's. I swear, sometimes they talk as if they've forgotten completely that it's a collection of their greatest hits played live.

"That's right," laughs Paul Raymond, reminded of the greatest live album accolade, bringing up something no one I know has ever noticed. "Joe Elliott says so, and Steve Harris... all those people. But I think the reason Michael left the band is that he thought the guitar sound on the live album was thin. I agree; it is quite thin, actually. It should have been recorded better, but it wasn't. I don't know, he just freaked out. Ron Nevison said, 'Well, that's it, there it is. That's all we can do with it; that's how it's come out.' Michael was very pissed-off about 'Rock Bottom' and the guitar sound. It wasn't fat enough. But I have to agree with it. But, you know, it's a five-man group and you just have to go along with it. No one else has complained about it. People enjoyed it, and Michael didn't notice it. It's all in the mind, isn't it? I think Michael, sometimes he looks just at himself and he doesn't see the overall picture, which is this band. People come and they still enjoy the songs. But the live album, the production was totally Nevison. In that department, you never get to put your oar in. With that record, it was kind of the sex, drugs and rock 'n' roll era. Guys are quite happy to just leave it. 'Ah, leave it to the producer!' (laughs). Let's go party."

Tens of thousands of fans of *Strangers in the Night* would disagree with most of what Paul just said there, and perhaps the truest thing uttered is that maybe it was all in Michael's mind. The record is drenched in power, and when most ardent students reflect upon that power, they are thinking squarely about the guitars.

"The third album, *Strangers in the Night*, the live album, it's a lot of people's favourite live album that they ever did," agrees Nevison. "I remember mixing at the Record Plant, mixing the album, the old Record Plant on Third Street in LA, and there was a French restaurant called Entourage next door, and I was in there having lunch, having a glass of wine, and a Sinatra song came on, 'Dooby dooby doo, strangers in the night.' 'Oh, *Strangers in the Night*, that would be a great title for this UFO thing.' It worked out great, like that. When Schenker left the group after the *Strangers in the Night* album, maybe my appetite for working with them... I don't even know if I was ever even offered another UFO, with the new line-up; I can't remember."

"But I do keep seeing that," says Nevison, reminded of the accolades in the live category album showered upon the record. "I still get feedback from fans, which is fairly nice. Schenker is such a great live guitar player, so it doesn't surprise me."

Yes indeed, overshadowing the success of the live album (about a dozen live records in the late '70s, including of course those mentioned above, virtually saved careers of many bands of UFO's stature) was the departure of one Michael Schenker, this time not for mere minutes on a moped, but for 15 years. But Michael indeed is on the live record, and Paul Chapman isn't, as Tonka himself explains.

"No, you know there's a huge controversy about that. No, I'm not on it. When I helped the band in 1977 for the *Lights Out* tour, and Michael showed up at Reading, when I was playing the Reading Festival with Lone Star, I said, 'You have to go back with your band. I can't be in two bands at the same time. One of them is in America and one of them is in Europe and it's fucking killing me. It's just brutal.' Anyway, so he went back with the band and they recorded *Obsession*, and then they went on the road and then I got a call in Wales from Wilf Wright, the band's manager, who somehow found me in a club I was playing at. This was fall of '78, and they said they were thinking of firing Michael, and would I be willing to move to LA and permanently be part of the band? Then they recorded the live album and Michael's antics were getting a little out of control—he was floating around LA doing something."

"Then anyway, the answer of course was yes," continues Paul, who would come on board for fully four UFO albums in the early '80s that are fast favourites of many knowledgeable and dedicated UFO fans. "The third Lone Star album had crashed and we had all sorts of management problems. Then I was in LA and Phil picked me up at the airport on Halloween of '78. They were still doing clean-ups on *Strangers in the Night* at The Record Plant, and it eventually came out in December of '78. I think Pete had a few bass cover-ups here and there and they were doing some mixing and whatnot. Two of the songs on there, which were on *Force It*, I had a major part in writing, which I wasn't credited for, 'Let It Roll' and 'Mother Mary,' and the thing about those, well, I can't bring in too much dirt here... I think those were studio tracks which were done with the crowd on, just to make it a full double album."

"So anyway," continues Tonka, "going back to The Record Plant, they were just finishing up and the first major tour I was going to do with UFO in America was opening for Rush, within about a week of me getting there. It was kind of like the start of the *Strangers in the Night* tour. That tour was fantastic, the first time I had ever seen Florida (note: Paul eventually moved there permanently). Well, that tour, in actual fact, I can remember sitting in the office. We didn't have the title for the album, so when the album came out it said 'Special thanks to our friend and guitarist Paul Chapman,' which was kind of a special thanks for when I helped them on the *Lights Out* tour. I think it was kind of covering any bridges in case—the actual credits were done before I was in the band—in case they needed to use me again, or if they wanted me in the band. Fortunately when the album actually did come out, I was in the band, so it was kind of justified. But a lot of people see that on there and think I had a large part of the actual playing of the album, which I didn't."

So to recap, Paul Chapman had played with the band as recently as the *Lights Out* tour, he is thanked on *Strangers in the Night*, and as soon as the band began "touring" *Strangers in the Night*, he was UFO's guitarist. It was a case of now you see him, blink, now you still see him. Hence the debate about Paul playing on the record.

Confirms Ron Nevison, "Paul Chapman, I've never met and I don't know who he is. He was the guitar player after me, so he had nothing to do with *Strangers in the Night*. No, he was not. We had a one guitar player band. We had Paul Raymond to play the guitar occasionally, when he wasn't playing keyboards. He was the guitar player/keyboard guy/background singer guy, in the band. Other than that, I mean, all the things I ever did with UFO involved the one guitar player, Schenker. I don't think that I ever used Paul Raymond as a guitar player in the studio. I think he played some guitar parts live, and probably he did some on *Strangers in the Night*."

That cleared up, Nevison does admit to some overdubbing on the record. "Well, I mean, yeah. I remember there being a confrontation with Schenker over something, but I remember it differently than Mike Clink remembers it. There was something that, either I wanted him to overdub something and he didn't want to do it, or he wanted to fix something and I said no; that's probably more like it. He probably wanted to fix something and I wouldn't let him fix it and he huffed out. But I don't think there was really that much overdubbing, to fix that album."

"We had recorded in Youngstown, Chicago, Columbus, I think maybe three, four shows, possibly Cleveland" recalls Ron. "So I picked takes that I wanted to use from those shows, but most of it was from one of the shows. I remember using the audience from Chicago because it was a bigger venue, and UFO was at that time very big in Chicago, although not a lot of the music was from Chicago. But that was one of their strongholds. I had no real concept of exactly what we were going to do when we finished the recording, but I do remember that we had enough material for a double album. We'd never really talked to Chrysalis about doing that, but when you have a song like 'Rock Bottom' that is ten minutes long, that's a quarter of the album. 'Love to Love' was another long live song. You know, seriously, you only have twenty minutes a side on vinyl. So all of a sudden we started talking about a double album. But we were like one or two songs short of doing that, so we went into the Record Plant and recorded two songs, and, you know, no one can tell."

As far as fun on the road goes, Paul recalls taking over a Grand Prix racetrack in Malibu on that Rush tour, and how everybody had to be Andy Parker for the day, because the drummer was the only one in the band with a driver's licence. However, the fun wasn't to last, as Pete ended up jumping in one of the cars and driving straight through the middle of the track rather than around it, getting the car stuck and hitting a fence, ultimately resulting in the band getting kicked out.

"Michael had a regimen," explains Tonka on further hijinks, offering some background on both of Michael's leavings, as well as a bit of the aftermath. "'At 6:00 in the morning, I must have two beers. At 7:00 in the morning, I must have two more beers and then at 8:15, I must have two Scotches and then I have the right feeling to play'—this kind of thing. So Michael is very German about his approach to consumption. But nothing was kind of out of order. But it was only then, when I got the call to help in 1977, they went around to Michael's apartment to pick him up, and he was gone and this is to do the *Lights Out* tour. The album is zooming up the Billboard 100 and it's like No.60 something and going up quickly and the tour is supposed to be starting and there is no Michael; nobody can find him."

"So they immediately called me and said, 'Help, help, help!' I'm like 'Oh, wait a minute.' I had just finished recording *Firing on All Six* with Lone Star. I mean, the first album did great all over Europe and we were supposed to be doing this album, we had a new management, we were supposed to be coming to America. The whole thing was in an up motion, and I said this is going to have to be temporary. Pete was saying, 'Well, can we just kind of borrow you like Thin Lizzy borrowed Gary Moore?' I said, 'Yes, but I have to come back. None of this trying to sway me.' I knew what was going to happen and I know how Pete and Phil are."

The mention of Gary Moore is pertinent here, as Moore was in fact considered as a replacement for Michael. The idea was actually floated to the Skid Row and Thin Lizzy legend, but Moore wound up turning the guys down.

"There were all these rumours about Michael joining the Moonies," continues Paul, referring to Michael's first escape at the time of *Lights Out*. "In actual fact Michael was going around Spain on a moped with his girlfriend just to get away from the pressure of everything. The pressure of being in a band that was starting to become successful was starting to eat at him a little bit. Anyway, that's when he came to see me in Reading and I told him you should go back with your band because I want to be with my band. Well at that point, they moved to LA, which is what they did—they were living in LA when I joined the band in 1977. But after Michael rejoined the band, they moved lock, stock and barrel and they did the whole Hollywood thing, had an office there. So I think that's when it kind of kicked in from an abuse point of view. *Lights Out* was being very successful, and then *Obsession*, which was recorded in LA, was doing great, and the peer pressure of newfound friends is pretty heavy, especially in LA. Everybody wants to get you high and everybody knows everybody else. Everybody is really cool and before you know it, there are a hundred people staying in your house. I know, because I moved there after that and it was exactly the same way. That's when Michael started going a little bit more bizarre."

But this time it had nothing to do with religious extremism. "No, as a matter of fact, far from it," says Chapman. "But then I joined UFO full-time and Michael started MSG and then I started hearing stories. We were staying in London and his wife came down. His next wife came down to talk to me about going to have a talk to him because he was staying in the rehearsal place and living in a flight case and he wouldn't go home. I said, 'What am I gonna do? I'm not a therapist. What am I, some kind of rock 'n' roll guitar counsellor?' Apart from the fact that we were getting in the car pretty much the next morning to go to Scotland or something. So I couldn't have done it anyway. I saw him quite a few times during that period. He came around my house on his birthday one time, just turned up out of the blue, and we went out."

"I mean... to live in a flight case and not go home," muses Paul on Michael's mental condition at the time. "I did hear rumours that he apparently burned his house down. Then there were certain things with the band where he was demanding things like, 'This person has to play here' and stuff with the label; there are 1001 of these things. But I don't want to throw dirt there, because I love Michael; he's a great guy. There was muck flying around in the press between Phil and Michael, Michael saying 'I'd never piss on him if he was on fire in the gutter' and Phil saying 'I'll never work with him again.' What you have to know is that in the music business, you can say whatever you want but nothing will ever surprise me. The thing with Michael was that he achieved some fantastic success on certain projects and other things."

Phil had taken to calling Michael "Michelle" in interviews, Mogg getting increasingly frustrated with Michael's drinking and erratic behaviour. As it turns out, Schenker's last show would be in Palo Alto, California, October of '78. "He just went," was Phil's amused assessment at the time. "He cracked up—we crack up a lot of people. Michael is on his own weird astral trip. His threshold of insanity is maybe a bit lower than anyone else's. He walks the line."

"They got me back for *Obsession*," says Michael offering his own version of events (and in effect saying that they got him back for the performances that would fill up *Strangers in the Night*), "and then in '78, we were mixing the live album. Actually, we were touring, I think, for the live album. Phil was a fighter, always fighting with people. I said to him one day, 'If you ever do this to me, I'm going to leave the band.' He punched me in the stomach to see if I really meant it, and I left. Just like in the Wild West. He thinks he's a cowboy or something (laughs). It was that simple."

"It was very easy at that point to go out and assemble musicians to play on the albums I wanted to make. So yes, he punched me in the stomach. I mean, I always did what I wanted. Nobody told me what to do. The only thing that was maybe a bit hard to take was that Phil wanted to be in charge of money and everything else. But for me, if I was playing the music I wanted, creatively, which was the most important thing for me, I did not let anybody in. Here is my song and you either like it or you don't. Phil and I... we'd just get along. We are musically connected and that's it. Also he is a rat and I am a horse, which is from the Chinese horoscope; total opposites, like ying and yang. Polarity-wise we are total opposites, like south and north."

Michael goes on to attempt comment on Tonka, now his replacement twice, as a guitarist. "I wouldn't know what I liked about him. I just know he was a good guitar player, at the time that we were playing, for what I knew about guitar playing, and in comparison to how far I had developed at that point in time. He had a certain style, but I don't know how original it was. To be honest, I don't really know. All I really know is that years later, when he was the guitarist in Waysted, I did not like the guitar playing. The guitar playing was the worst part of that band. So at that point, I guess I had developed and understood what I wanted. I guess what he was doing didn't fit in with my tastes."

"I'm not sure of *Strangers in the Night*," reflected Michael in 1988, shifting the blame back onto himself. "Maybe I was too close and too sceptical about my own performance. I always think I could have chosen a better take. It's incredible how many people think that was one of the best live albums. I personally didn't think so. It had a very good sound, but I think I had better takes somewhere or could've done a better take. But *Lights Out* was the first incredibly produced album I'd been involved with. There were excellent songs and Ron Nevison did an incredible job. It was the first big success for me."

"Michael makes his own problems," sighs Pete. "It wouldn't matter if, bless him... because I like Michael very much. But if you had a bloody leaf fall out of a tree, he'd get into a problem and panic. So you never really know what goes on in Michael. But Michael and I did an album called *The Plot* that Michael and I really enjoy. I enjoy Michael's enthusiasm. Unfortunately, we're not particularly normal. You know, I didn't sign... if I was going to be normal, I'd be doing something different."

Pete's reaction to Michael's "reasons" for leaving the band at various times elicits an "I don't know. I don't really take much notice, to be truthful. I mean, if you say to me, roundabout those sorts of times, that might be when I was into getting some coke or trying to withdraw from heroin addiction. I find those sorts of things are so... you know, you either plug in and play or you don't. Or you fuck off, you know what I mean? Don't you think it's a bit theatrical? You know, I can't imagine Richard Burton or Lawrence Olivier... you know, same sort of thing. Yeah, sure you're playing with the best, but at the same time, you know, that's what you did! It's not like he'd been a plumber or worked at McDonald's. That's what he did. That's why you've got great soccer players. I'll say this. People ride the pressure and they actually go on and achieve. It's a bit like, you should say, 'Well, actually myself and my colleagues have done very, very well,' and that's why you do have colleagues. In a band. That's why it's a gang. You're going around with the best gang in the world."

But we're in fact talking about some sort of mental unbalance here. "Mmm, it's very difficult to deal with that. For instance, you can only give so much support with that. Because after awhile it becomes boring."

Finally Pete, as expected, puts a different spin on the "he punched me" story. "Well, that was... you know what? It's funny, but it comes up this one time. That was over... somebody had taken the last downer; Michael had it. That was in Belgium. Actually it was a onetime thing. I wasn't even there. But it was a bit like, you know, this goes back to the thing, 'Well, who's got the drugs?' Michael ate the last one. Suddenly there's an argument. In the sober world of sanity, you go, 'Well, I was drunk. I'm sorry, on that.' Vice versa. Two people are drunk; who even knows? For me, I can't stand people who are arrogant. Arrogance is stupidity. So when you ask about something like that, well then, the two of them were probably arrogant and stupid at the time and they should grow up."

"I've heard this kind of stuff from him and it's old news," scoffs Phil, years later, referring to the same fateful incident. "He's left the band half a dozen times, he's left the Scorpions twice and he's even left his own band. Whatever the excuse or reason is, it's always someone else's fault. He's somebody who doesn't take responsibility for his actions. As I recall—and I could be wrong—he wasn't actually hit, he was shoved. There's a lot of difference and the reason for that was due to a financial deal that he'd gone and done when we'd put all the money into the band. This was very early on when we were buying equipment. He was like a fuckin' storm in a teacup. It almost makes me feel like not responding because for someone to hold onto that for so many years, something that is so childish, it's almost crazy. I believe Michael left during the mixing of *Strangers*. He's left a few times; I've lost track. Unfortunately once we got into the '80s, we started to spiral a little bit out of control."

"There's been so much madness associated with Michael," continues Phil. "It's an endless thing; you could probably spend a couple of days going through it. It would go on forever (laughs). I love Michael's playing and 80% of him is really good. The other part of him is that he has a rather unfortunate side; you just have to look at his actions. I don't have to justify the band or anything else."

Andy Parker, speaking with Marko Syrjala, summarizes all of this for us, most pertinently going over Paul Chapman's various roles to this point and beyond. "Right, exactly, so Paul was in the band first as a second guitar player. After we recorded the *Phenomenon* album, Michael had 'Doctor Doctor' with a double lead in it, and when we had to take that on the road he said it was going to be difficult for him to do it, so maybe we would have to think about getting another guitar player to play the rhythm and the extra lead. So we did auditions and we got Paul Chapman. As it turned out it didn't work out very well, because it was like putting two cooks into one kitchen; it was a bit too much."

"After that we went back to a four-piece and decided that maybe a keyboard player would be better. That's when we got Danny Peyronel and did *No Heavy Petting*. Danny was great, but he had more of an ego of a solo kind of guy, so that's when we got Paul Raymond and Paul worked perfectly. He's so underrated, the guy sings, he plays guitar, he plays keyboards, he's just great. The line-up with Phil, Pete, Michael, Paul and me, I think it was just a great line-up."

"Then Paul Chapman came in again when Michael disappeared overnight, because we knew him. Paul did that American tour for us, for which we were all very grateful. Then of course Michael came back and did the *Strangers in the Night* album. He said he'd come in and do the live album and then he'd be gone. The last part of the tour was the British tour and then Michael left. Paul came back in and we did some good albums. You had *No Place to Run, The Wild, The Willing and the Innocent, Mechanix* and *Making Contact*—great albums."

"You have to understand that from 1974 to 1979, Michael got in there and he worked," qualifies Andy. "We toured continuously, we toured the States and he did a lot of work. It just got too much for him, I think, and I do understand. It's not the life for everybody, being on the road for months on end away from your family; it's not easy. So I do understand the problem. But when you're in a band there are a lot of people relying on you. It's not just the guys in the band, it's the crew, it's the lights, it's the sound, it's the agents, it's the managers, the people that pay to get the ticket. It's a serious thing and you've got to make a commitment."

"I have to say he got worse over the years. But he'd done a good four years, when we had *Phenomenon, Force It* and *No Heavy Petting* and we had toured with them continuously. Michael worked really hard and he was great. I'm gonna tell you one thing, and I don't tell this to many people, he's the only guitar player—and I can't remember where the show was—but I remember that we were playing and he was soloing and his solo was so amazing that I stopped playing. I kind of lost it because I was listening to him on the monitor and that tells you just how good the guy was."

Pete goes on to confront the subject of UFO and drugs from pre-Michael to Michael leaving the fold. "You know, we grew up in an era where people were smoking pot and things like that. I did acid when I was like 15, lots of it. Then, of course, as soon as we got to America, at the time, cocaine was everywhere. Record company people, they would say, 'What do you want? You wanna got for a meal or do you want some coke?' So we did cocaine all the time. I did it to the point where, when I had no money, I'd do coke, on the road, because I enjoyed it. I'm not saying anything great about drugs, but to a certain extent, they create an environment that made us feel a little bit different. Then again, you start to earn enough money to buy as much coke as you want."

"Now, actually, I drink, and I look at that, because there's not much point... I can do a line or I can do an ounce, and what's the point, really? You'd done it, seen it, and certainly I wouldn't say it enhances my performance. In actual fact, for people that come and watch me play, these days I'll concentrate on my performance as opposed to how much... I don't regard substance as substance abuse. I actually think of it as sometimes you need it. At night, I like things like that. But not anymore though. If you're in the middle of Iowa or something like that, bored stiff, and you want to chat and you're having a really good time, it works perfectly."

As for the rest of the band, Way says, "I don't think with UFO there was a problem, to be truthful. Because at that time, you know, like, staying up until six in the morning with a few grams of coke wasn't actually too much of a problem. I think it was great. It actually kept the band on the road. You're hanging out with your colleagues. You're hanging out with your mates, doing a line, having a few drinks, talking about things. But, certainly I wouldn't recommend it. 'Get a band together; first thing you need is cocaine.' Actually, the last thing you need is cocaine! That would be my comment."

"We were all pretty bad," says Andy. "We had such a reputation. I haven't really thought about it. When you are inside the band, you never really think about a reputation, the way other people perceive you. We were a pretty hard-drinking, hard-partying band, for a long time. I still like a drink, but not like the old days. I mean, it just used to be insane. Sun up until sundown. I guess I was almost at the top of the list, I don't know, maybe third or fourth. Somewhere in the middle."

"Touring for two years non-stop is sometimes not much fun," adds Pete. "So we had to make our own fun, using lots and lots of cocaine and drinking. It was like being a schoolboy. We went to have a good time, we didn't care who we played with or how we did it. We were getting more and more successful; the albums were selling very well in America and reasonably well in Europe. It was like a schoolboy being let into a candy store, as I said. We managed to get on a lot of people's nerves. We felt that we were the best band around and we didn't care what band we played with. That's when we were playing as special guests to a lot of really big bands. We could play with Aerosmith for instance who were really big in America at the time and we could go down just as well as them and later on we did our own shows for 10,000, 15,000 people with AC/DC as our special guest. It was a good time. If you played and played and played, you had so much confidence and it was a reward to see what we thought was the quality of our music being seen by a lot of people. And don't forget, no hit singles, just albums."

In any event, drugs or not, the band sounded fired up on the sonic snapshot in time that was *Strangers in the Night*. The album opened with a rousing, cohesive, fat, celebratory "Natural Thing," which gave way to a delightful, melodic "Out in the Street," followed by a casual, friendly "Only You Can Rock Me," keyboards in full bloom. "Doctor Doctor" closes side one, this version being the best recording of the track through to this day, the song galloping with full power, killer guitar sound, just the right incestuous blend between the instrumentation metaphorically evoking the alchemy and majesty of the band's keyboard-with-three-piece chemistry.

UFO were finally rewarded with a Top 40 hit on home soil when "Doctor Doctor" was issued as a picture sleeve single on clear vinyl, backed with "On with the Action" live from the same tour, 1978, and the studio version of "Try Me." The song was also issued as a single in the US, backed with "Lights Out," as well as in Germany, backed with "On with the Action." The galloping Schenker anthem would continue to live on through its perennial presence in UFO sets long after Michael was gone, as well as its use as the intro music for that most galloping of heavy metal bands of the '80s, Iron Maiden. That band's dear leader and bassist Steve Harris has never denied the huge impact Pete Way has had on him, from his stage presence to his fashion sense, and he, along with Slash from Guns N' Roses, have long extolled the virtues of *Strangers in the Night*. "Doctor Doctor" reached No.35 in the UK charts, helping push the album to No.7, while in the US, the album managed a No.42 placement.

Side two finds "Mother Mary" fully actualized and electrified (although, as alluded to above, this was recorded in a studio!), while "This Kid's" features curiously clean guitar for the main riff and again, very pronounced keyboard tones—curious, again, until we find out that it is the other song, besides "Mother Mary," that was deviously cooked up back at The Record Plant, November of 1978.

"Love to Love" closes the side, this demanding track winning through accurate, thoughtful production choices, namely, again, sonically well-placed keyboards, which of course are dream-weavingly integral to the song. It must be said as well, that Andy Parker is a big part of this record's forcefulness. The songs rock because he is raucous and then they are recorded by Nevison richly on all frequencies.

Side three offers the band's two sister tracks, "Lights Out" and "Rock Bottom," two tracks that are ironically two of the band's biggest—I say ironically, because they are also two of UFO's heaviest and fastest. "Lights Out" is presented in full metallic glory, rhythm guitar back-track from Paul Raymond actually sounding louder than Schenker (who has a point—for the most part, his solos are buried), while "Rock Bottom" represents the album's only old school live album unravelling, the track becoming an 11-minute monster housing a jazzy jam over which Michael gets to noodle.

Side four finds the band blazing out strong, offering three rockers in "Too Hot to Handle," "Let It Roll" (okay, way too much keyboard on this one) and finally the pubby and chummy "Shoot Shoot," with arguable emotional highpoint "I'm a Loser" arriving second track in. It's fitting that "Shoot Shoot" might just mark the biggest high octane improvement over its paired studio original of all on here, the band really slamming it home, grinding the groove, sounding like an unmatchable bar band at a magic packed gig to remember.

"Shoot Shoot" would also be issued as a picture sleeve, clear vinyl single in the UK. backed with "Only You Can Rock Me" and "I'm a Loser," the track made it to No.48 on the UK charts. *Strangers in the Night* would be reissued in 1999, expanding to include renditions of "Hot 'n' Ready" and "Cherry," which served to remind the listener how *Obsession* as a record wound up a bit of a passed-over cold fish.

"Chrysalis did the launch for the album and they rented out The Planetarium in LA," recalls Nevison. "It was called the Griffith Observatory, in Griffith Park. That is where we did the launch party and it was very cool. Pretty sure that was for *Strangers in the Night*; it was for one of them and I don't think it was for the other two. As far as rumours of them not liking each other, I don't think that's true. Not on the three albums I did with them. I didn't find that. I mean Schenker was a loner. He really didn't hang out with them. I didn't find any kind of dislike. They never showed that to me. The falling out they had was after I worked with them, after I did the *Strangers in the Night* album.

"I think the main reason that album sounds so good is that we had done *Phenomenon, Force It, No Heavy Petting, Lights Out* and *Obsession* before that," opines Phil, looking back. "We had been doing an awful lot of touring, a lot of work in Europe and America. We'd done a lot of shows with Rush and Cheap Trick so when we did the live album it came right at the crest of that wave. All the work had been put in and it was a combination of all the best songs that we had been playing live. I think it has to be the right time when you do a live album and for us it was the right time."

"I love the *Strangers* album, always have done," adds Andy. "Because I always felt that UFO never really came across in the studio, as they did a live band. It was probably the way we were forced to spend all our time on the road, write, get in, make an album. We were never really that prepared for it. So you always had to struggle a bit in the studio, putting it together. It wasn't until a song came into the live set and we played it for a while, all of a sudden it started to sound like UFO. That's why I love that *Strangers* album because it really was UFO, everything UFO was. But getting Michael in, '73, '74, and that whole thing where we went and signed with Chrysalis and did these albums, *Phenomenon, Force it, No Heavy Petting*, the band was just on a curve and an upward wave. Everything was coming together and getting better and better. Finally with *Strangers*, I had something in my hand that really sounded like the band."

"I actually like the feeling of spontaneity in our shows," says Pete, on UFO as a live force. "Some bands today, so-called rock 'n' roll bands, are so safe and predictable and a lot of them are only doing it for the money, and it makes me sick to see these idiots in magazines in hard rock bands who used to be into pop or cabaret. The one thing no one can ever accuse UFO of is having sold out. It's something our record company could never understand, why were we selling out 20,000-seater arenas in America, but because of their lack of understanding, never receiving the kind of support someone like Debbie Harry got. People from the record company then never came to our shows; they didn't like us! They'd rather snort coke instead. One American tour we did, the 'medical bill' was over $20,000! We've no regrets, though, because it's the way we choose to live, even though it did get wildly out of order. That's what I'm trying to say, though, yes, we were wrecked for a lot of it, we destroyed drugs like you wouldn't believe, but we were still beating everyone else. Live, no one could touch us. The only ones who gave us a run for our money were AC/DC with Bon Scott."

Reflected Phil at the time, speaking with the legendary Harry

Doherty, now passed on, "We began our career by starting in England, doing clubs, and then going off to Germany playing halls. We went to America and spent three years breaking through there, and then we came back to England—which suddenly started to pick up after *Lights Out*. So we really had three careers within one."

Asked to defend against charges of being unfashionable for the times, Mogg says, "Unfashionable from whose point of view? From a press point of view? Well, it was only two years ago that we ever did an interview. We never employed the services of a PR before that. There was never any contact made, so we never bothered. As long as we could go out and do our gig and reasonably fill a place, and then come back and fill it even more, we were quite happy with that. I think we had a big thing against hype and against anything that wasn't reasonably honest. That's what steered us clear of meeting the right people. I think we're glad that we didn't take the correct paths, so to speak. In every manner, from signing contracts, etc., we sort of did it arse-upwards. But, as we see, it works itself out in the end."

On the subject of how closely Phil identifies with his audience, Mogg said, "Well, I always enjoy going to gigs. I never think I'm with the kids. I don't think of myself as being one of the kids. Anyway, merely saying 'We are with the kids' detaches them from it in the first place. By saying that, it's putting you on a different plateau immediately. A lot of bands reason these things out for themselves and convince themselves of the situation they're in. They work out a philosophy in their minds that justifies their existence."

"But you also get a lot of journalists getting so much in depth about the whole thing that you lose sight of the main object, which is playing and enjoying yourself. I know what 'enjoying yourself' sounds like. Awful. But that's the basis of it. When I used to go out after work, it was to enjoy myself. A lot of people work out the whys and wherefores of the whole business. I spoke to one guy and he was saying, 'Why do you do it?' I said that it was good fun, laughs, and he was saying, 'Yes, but if you were doing a nine-to-five job, would you think the same thing?' I did work a nine-to-five job and that was good fun too. You find the good fun there, like nailing the shop steward's shoes to the floor or sewing his trousers up."

"We've always believed in enjoying ourselves," added Pete, in the same Melody Maker feature. "I could never relate to bands who go to gigs and have just half a lager. In fact, there's a lot of bands that I know that don't even drink before they play. I find that very strange. Dunno if it's because I get off on drinking before I play. We've actually always got out of it when we go on the road. It keeps us going."

Asked by Harry if the band winds up staying up all night on the road, Pete adds, "Ah, well, a lot of it depends whether the coke's cut with speed or with laxitol. Nah, it's usually about four o'clock as a rule. The sevens and eights are real grinders. They don't happen so much. But we actually need and enjoy touring. I think that if you're not on the road for any period, you start to become detached from what's actually going on. It's very difficult to go and do an album without being on the road. That, to me, has been a part of rock 'n' roll. It's the whole, as opposed to the segments, that we enjoyed."

Doing well in America and, as alluded to, somewhat being based in California at the time, the band was starting to generate a fair bit of press in the US. Goldmine magazine asked Phil about the differences between European and American audiences, Mogg explaining that, "The European fan is mainly, from our point of view, a rock 'n' roll heavy metal fan. In England we saw maybe eight women on the whole of our tour. It's all men. In America the women are up for as much as the men. You get a whole 50/50 audience. I would think in America the audiences are a lot wilder; there's a lot more whooping. We had our share of experiences with audiences. In Germany, one time, having too much to drink, I took on one of the audience and the whole place went mad. We carried on playing after and did manage to miss the bottles. That was a bit scary. It was a long time ago, before we grew up. It was a very silly gig. I had a fight with the guy. This particular person kept opening his mouth so I went down into the audience and we had a bit of a rough house. Then after, the audience went wild. The way I see it, having been through it all, it's really dangerous, actually. Look at what the fans did to the Jefferson Starship equipment when the band couldn't play. Jeff Beck too. The German audiences really get out of hand."

Asked by Smith to describe the average UFO fan, Mogg questions, "Is that male or female? Girls fall into lots of categories, don't they? We seem to get the ages 16 to 20. I think the guys are out for the rock, mainly. Girls are out for anything, I suppose. We don't see an awful lot, but I must admit, it's hard for them to get backstage. We have tight security. The guys I speak to are into guitars and sound. The girls are into other things."

"The lesson to be learned from this album is undoubtedly that the natural habitat of a heavy metal band is in concert," wrote Harry Doherty, in his review of *Strangers in the Night* for Melody Maker. "The proof comes when the coldness and relative inefficiency of UFO's studio work is placed alongside the roasting live hive of hard rock activity on *Strangers in the Night*. Tracks that sounded mediocre in the studio suddenly come to life in live performance. Players whose grasp of technique could at best be termed 'adequate' in the confines of a recording booth are magically transformed into heroes when faced with an adoring audience, and respond to that adulation magnificently. Listening to *Strangers in the Night* you begin to comprehend why UFO are (a) a fast-growing cult in the UK and (b) such a massive attraction in America. They do the right. They feed their audiences on the staple diet of the lowest common denominator: the riff, the solo, the vocal. And when a band does that as well as UFO do on this album, then criticism is beside the point."

Closing his assessment, Doherty opines that, "The momentum rarely lets up, but I can't help thinking that it would've been a superior proposition as a single album. Come side three, UFO lose touch with the fact that they're at their most potent as a solid unit and lapse into the inevitable solo antics with Schenker's mediocre solo on 'Rock Bottom,' and it's not until the third track on the final side, 'Let It Roll,' that the heat picks up again. Still, I doubt if their diehard fans will agree. They'll take as much as they're given. On *Strangers in the Night*, they're certainly given as much as they can take."

"How about this for a paradox?" asks the NME's Bob Edmands. "Here's a high-energy heavy metal band that display's fine taste and judgment. UFO's riffs are exhilarating without ever being overbearing. Michael Schenker's guitar solos are flashily attacking but don't outstay their welcome. And Phil Mogg's vocals are suitably rich and raucous without resorting to caricature."

"No doubt they'll get disgustingly rich on the strength of *Strangers*," concludes Edmands, reflecting the spiteful punk—or by this point, post-punk—times. "But that's true of all successful rock performers—buy an album, support the wealthy. If you're into rock music, you have to live with such social implications. That UFO have long hair and live in California makes them no less entitled to their moolah than your friendly neighbourhood spikey-heads. Inevitably, *Strangers* is an album that will be deeply unfashionable. But if trendies are foolish enough to neglect it, that's their business."

Bloodied but unbowed, Phil was proud of what he had achieved with UFO across the decade thus far, telling Trouser Press the year *Strangers in the Night* came out, "There is nothing—and I mean nothing—preconceived about UFO, not even our name. It is more likely to our disadvantage to be so carefree, but UFO is trying to bring the human element back into rock. We want audience excitement and response to be an intuitive reaction to the band, not because of an elaborate stage show or a few explosions. As an opening act, we've got fifty minutes to gig. We've got to come out and hit them and hit them hard! It's tremendously aggressive for us being on stage. We don't want to carry that aggressiveness around with us all day."

"We only need to satisfy ourselves," continues Mogg. "We're one band who wants no regrets. There'll be no saying later that we shouldn't have done this or done that. I don't know what our image is, nor do I have any idea what I want it to be. That's why we're a looser organization than many. We go through a series of sagas every day. You know, half out of it, missing planes, checking into wrong hotels. I'm no longer surprised with anything about UFO."

Epilogue

"UFO lived the rock 'n' roll lifestyle to the very max"

After a hat trick of records in both the American and UK charts, UFO found themselves without their golden egg. Michael Schenker was now gone, with the inevitable brought in as replacement. As discussed, Paul "Tonka" Chapman had worked with the band post-*Phenomenon* and pre-*Force It*, also contributing with live dates on the *Strangers in the Night* tour, if you buy the fact that a live album can have a tour.

"There were always different people considered, but nothing really went anywhere with anybody else," says Phil on adopting Chapman into the ranks of UFO post-Michael. "We were always a bit of an insular band. It was kind of the people you grew up with and the people you played with. It was even a bit of a wrench when Andy left. We were always one of those bands where it's better the devil you know. I don't think it's a great idea anyway to get somebody who is predominantly known. When Michael left and we got Paul Chapman in, we could have gone out and got some antsy fancy name, but it was better to have somebody in the band who was going to be a band mate, a band player, somebody you knew. Michael is more insular and Paul's an extrovert, so it was from one extreme to another. In terms of tension, no, that was later, in the mid '80s. Those years became known as the years of excess, didn't they? Not success—excess. I think we did our fair share of that course."

"A bit difficult with Paul," notes Paul Raymond, years later summing up his relationship with Chapman. "Very different sort of character. He's not as dedicated to his practice and his music as Michael."

"Paul's a great guitar player," mused Pete, decades later, speaking with Rich Davenport. "He performs always; he was an ace player. He could play. To replace Michael is pretty much impossible, isn't it? He did a damn good job of making it like a good rock 'n' roll band. He was a really good guitar player. More in the Gary Moore mould, actually, than Michael. Because Michael was the king of one or two notes, making you want to cry when you hear him, you know what I mean?"

But Paul was indestructible; hence the aforementioned nickname "Tonka." "Well, that goes back around the '80s, when the heroin thing started, and the drink thing," says Chapman, elaborating on the etymology. "It was always a drink thing, but in Lone Star, and even in early UFO, it was always... everyone smoked dope; it was what you did. It was like, when everybody else would be so passed-out, the only one that doesn't have a driving licence is me, and I would be the one that had to drive across Scandinavia. This kind of thing. And I'd have to be the one that checked us into the hotel or got the boat tickets to get the band on the boat."

"Phil started saying, 'He's indestructible. He's like one of those things that you wind up. What do you call them toys?' Somebody said, 'Tonka toys!' 'Yeah,' he said, 'that's it.' So we were coming back down the M1 and I'm driving the Range Rover and he's in the back throwing up or something like that, and he's supposed to be driving. He's like, 'Well done, Tonka!' I think Ross Halfin was there or Gary Bushell was there or somebody was there and it ended up in print and from then on it just kind of stuck. In the end, you bump into people like Joe Elliott, 'Hey Tonka, how's it going?' It wasn't even Paul anymore. So it was the indestructible thing. Well, that's how it was then. It's not like that anymore. You get old and you calm down a bit."

Where was the now-exiled Mr. Schenker while Paul was on board burning up stages in support of *Strangers in the Night*? Well, he had rejoined his brother Rudolf in Scorpions for that band's scorching sixth album *Lovedrive*, issued in January of 1979, same month *Strangers in the Night* hit the shops in America.

"What happened was that I had just left UFO," explains Michael, on the strange turn of events. "My brother heard about it. The Scorpions were just bringing in a new guitarist. My brother wanted me to play on parts of the new album. He gave me a tape and I went into the studio and played it. It went down so well that they asked me to join. I was already worn out but because it was my brother, I decided to forget about all those things. Also, I forgot that if I were to play live with them then they would play a whole lot of songs from records they made before *Lovedrive*. I was going to have to copy all of those songs. I felt like, 'What am I doing here?' I was copying and playing Uli Roth's stuff. I like to keep the highlights and improvise the rest. I could not do that. I found myself in an unhappy place."

"Plus I was afraid of touring," continues Schenker. "When *Lights Out* made it into the charts, I got so scared that I would have to constantly tour that I just sold everything and went away. So, it goes without saying that what happened with the Scorpions was a similar situation. I had very bad stage fright. I was taking prescription tablets so that I could go onstage. I was taking them before I went on instead of drinking, but then I started taking the tablets and drinking together. It was too much of an effort and too much of a nuisance. I asked myself, 'What am I doing here? Why have I chosen this profession?'"

"God has his own way of making you strong. I think there was a reason why I had to go that way. What you are most afraid of comes right at you. I learned the hard way to lose my shyness and I grew out of it. I could not even make interviews back then. I remember one time they switched a tape on and the guy left the room and left me sitting there with the tape on. I was only 18. Phil was next door and he wondered why he didn't hear anything. I was just looking at the tape rolling. The guy comes back and says, 'How did it go?' I was like, 'How did what go?' He couldn't understand why I didn't say anything. Most people have a lot to say, even when they are not asked. He thought I was like that, but I was not. I would only say something when someone asked me a question. I would never talk."

"I missed out on ten years of social skills because I was too busy being creative," reflects Michael, on the long and action-packed journey that led him into Scorpions, in and out of UFO, back into Scorpions and back out again. "I was like a big movie star who was always working and missed out on his son's first baby steps. I had no idea how to be social or how to behave. Most of what I have learned about being social I have learned since I have been in the United States. I moved here in 1989. I have been to a lot of self-improvement programs. I am much happier now that I'm not so shy. Life is more fun and flows much easier. I think that is why my guitar playing is flowing better. I used to play so tense that it would slow me down. I would try so hard and I was actually getting slower. I would hit the string harder than I would need to and I would press down harder than I would need to. I would be worn-out after two solos."

When asked whether his brother was angry when Michael quit the band, Schenker says that, "It hurt him. He probably thought I was playing with him or being an egotistical person. People didn't understand what I was suffering from. I knew that if I told them, 'I can't do this. Please get Matthias Jabs back. I have to leave,' that they would have talked me into staying. I was easily manipulated. I was always the youngest member in the band by six or eight years; I would just follow the pack. They didn't understand that I suffered from panic attacks. I started having them when I was 15 years old. They didn't really understand what my health condition was and where I was in my head. I think it hurt them a lot but I don't think they ever really understood the truth about the whole thing."

"I was kind of in limbo land not knowing what my next step was going to be. As I say, when I did the *Lovedrive* album everyone was so impressed and they really persuaded me to join the band and they got rid of Matthias, basically. I did a little bit of the tour and I realised that I could not do this. I had done this, and I had been there, but there was something else that I needed to do but I couldn't figure out yet what it was. I was invited to audition for Aerosmith and stuff like that. I kind of disappeared from the tour because I couldn't talk to them as I knew they would try to persuade me to stay. I just couldn't. Matthias freaked out and he left again and they asked me again and I said, 'I can't do this, honestly, I can't do this.' They said, 'Please, please, please.' I tried again but I just couldn't do it. I couldn't stand on stage, night after night, copying other people's lead breaks."

Michael was also in the running to replace Randy Rhoads in Ozzy's band after the LA axe legend's tragic death in a fly-by prank on the road. There was also the idea to form a new band with Denny Carmassi and Bill Church, the rhythm section of the classic Montrose line-up. Eventually what happened, of course, was The Michael Schenker Group, who issued a fetching and spirited self-titled debut album in August of 1980, like UFO, recording for Chrysalis. Although Roger Glover produced the record, Michael would reunite with Ron Nevison for the sophomore album, with old mate Paul Raymond also coming on board.

"Eventually, in 1980, I understood what was happening," reflects Michael. "My brother's vision was to make it all the way to the top with a band. It was his dream but it wasn't my dream. I am a lead guitarist who needs musical freedom. Matthias eventually joined for good and they found somebody who was pulling on the same string and that was important. I always tell my brother that he would have never been able to experience what he experienced because I would not have been pulling on the same string, as I have a totally different dream than he has."

As for UFO, they moved onto some very productive years with Paul Chapman commanding the guitar position, occasional help from Paul Raymond, soon to be replaced by Neil Carter. Considered UFO classics are 1980's *No Place to Run* and 1981's *The Wild, The Willing and the Innocent.* Also solid are 1982's *Mechanix* and 1983's *Making Contact.* What must be said is that Phil's reputation as a lyricist is made across these records and not the songs of the '70s. For whatever reason, as the '80s began, Phil became twice as imagistic and twice the storyteller.

After fits and starts with the line-ups through the balance of the '80s and '90s, the band is still thriving today, having settled in with American guitarist Vinnie Moore for fully five studio records of original material at this point.

"I think the production with Ron Nevison was very important for us," notes Pete, looking back. "Ron and us together at the same time was perfect. He caught the style. I mean, he had worked with Led Zeppelin, Bad Company, some very good people and he was able to capture us live but make it sophisticated and fresh. After that, they're very difficult albums to follow-up. I would say writing with Paul Chapman was different as well, because it changed the attitude of the writing. It's difficult to put into words, but I would say there are some very good songs on them, but they weren't produced by Ron Nevison. George Martin's a lovely man, but he didn't really capture our rock 'n' roll sound in the same way. It was a lot smaller sound. It wasn't the rock thing that I like and I think we get with Ron. Ron could make it sound clean, but also make it powerful. But the Chapman era albums were good and people still ask for those songs."

There's a hundred guys who will tell you much the same sorts of tales about UFO, but Steve Dawson of Saxon fame can add a bunch of personal experience—and affection—to the telling.

"Sure, I've always loved UFO, and I'm proud to say that Pete Way is a great friend of mine," chuckles Dawson. "We supported UFO many times—but in America, oddly—and Pete is one of my greatest influences. I just love that guy. He's just one of the best ever bass players/front men ever. I must say, I nicked a few things off him myself in my act. But there are plenty of things to tell about Pete because obviously UFO lived the rock 'n' roll lifestyle to the very max."

"When we were on tour with them, in America, on one of the last tours that we did, they had got a new manager who was trying to stop them drinking and taking illegal substances. There was no drinking in their dressing rooms or anything like that, but obviously they found out we'd got plenty of what they wanted, so they were in our dressing room all the time. If you went to the toilet, Pete would have been looking over your shoulder saying, 'What are you doing?' Thinking you were going to do something that he wanted (laughs). Just really funny."

"I mean, we played in Chicago and I think that was their biggest city in America. We played this massive place, and by this time the drink ban had been well squelched, if you know what I mean. They were just doing what they wanted, and Pete went on and first song, threw his bass right up in the air, but forgot he'd thrown it, I think (laughs). It just came down and smashed to pieces (laughs). But that's how they are and I love them for that. I think they're a great band. Recently, a few years back, we did the big biker show in England called the Bulldog Bash, and it was Motörhead, UFO and us and obviously Pete Way was not with them but Phil Mogg was there and we had a good chat and a few beers after."

As for memories of Paul Chapman, who would steer the ship through the early '80s, Dawson says, "What I remember about him is that he was the butt of a lot of jokes (laughs). They made fun of him. Because what it is? UFO are from the west country in England, and they have like a really funny way of speaking, and what probably didn't seem funny to them was hilarious to us. They were just making jokes about Tonka all the time. But he was a brilliant guitarist, absolutely fantastic. But, having said that, I don't think you can beat the Michael Schenker version—that is just the classic UFO. I remember going to see them at Sheffield City Hall, thinking, fuck, listen to this—this is what I want to be like and that's it. Tonka is a great guitarist. I don't know what he's doing now, because when we did the show with them, he wasn't with them. It was Paul Raymond and Vinnie Moore, who's also a great guitarist, absolutely."

"But when we played with them at the beginning there, you couldn't touch UFO. They were doing across the board. In towns where they were really popular, they did big hockey arenas, yeah, but otherwise, they would do small theatres that might hold 2,000. I think by then things were getting difficult for them. But no matter what, they played absolutely great. No problems whatsoever. But the offstage antics were brilliant. They were fantastic."

Again, there was always Pete and his classic look—Pete Way made bass playing cool. "Oh for sure, in his stripy trousers, and generally being up front, where if you're that type of personality, you want to be like that. The role is mostly pretty secondary. A lot of bass players in the past would just stand at the back and do the job. But that's not ever what I wanted to do, and when I saw Pete Way, it influenced me, it made me think anything was possible. I don't want to speak for him, but I think it must've influenced Steve Harris as well, because he's the same age as me, and UFO were a band that was signed up and making records before we were. So you look at guys like Pete and say, I want to be like that. That's probably still how it is today, I should imagine (laughs)."

Discography

A. 1970 - 1979

This is primarily a UK discography, i.e. discography of "first issue," given that UFO are a British band. UK issue is used for spellings and punctuation of song titles, timings and credits. I've used the notes section as a sort of free-form area to bring up limited additional points I considered salient. Personnel is only addressed at the outset and then when a change is made. This is the only place songs aren't in double quote marks (or single, when toggled inside of speaker quotations).

1

(Beacon BEAS 12, Oct. '70)

Side 1: 1. Unidentified Flying Object (UFO) 2:47; 2. Boogie for George (UFO) 4:15; 3. C'mon Everybody (Cochran, Capehart) 3:10; 4. Shake It About (UFO) 3:46; 5. (Come Away) Melinda (Hellerman/Minkoff) 4:49

Side 2: 1. Timothy (UFO) 3:28; 2. Follow You Home (Way) 2:10; 3. Treacle People (Bolton) 3:24; 4. Who Do You Love (McDaniel) 7:48; 5. Evil (Way) 3:27

Notes: Other significant issues include German Teldec, Decca and Nova, US Rare Earth and Japanese Stateside. "(Come Away) Melinda" listed as "Melinda" on back cover. Personnel: Phil Mogg – vocals; Mick Bolton – guitars; Pete Way – bass; Andy Parker – drums.

2: Flying

(Beacon BEAS 19, Oct. '71)

Side 1: 1. Silver Bird (UFO) 6:45; 2. Star Storm (UFO) 18:50; 3. Prince Kajuku (UFO) 3:55

Side 2: 1. The Coming of Prince Kajuku (UFO) 3:35; 2. Flying (UFO) 26:30

Notes: Most significant issues are German Teldec, Decca and Nova and Japanese Stateside. Arguably, the title also includes the words One Hour Space Rock.

Live

(Decca SLK-16769, '72)

Side 1: 1. C'mon Everybody (Cochran, Capehart) 4:10; 2. Who Do You Love (McDaniel) 9:00; 3. Loving Cup (Butterfield) 5:10

Side 2: 1. Prince Kajuku/The Coming of Prince Kajuku (UFO) 8:20; 2. Boogie for George (UFO) 11:30; 3. Follow You Home (Way) 6:00
Notes: Live album recorded in Japan. Most significant issues include German Teldec, Decca and Nova and Japanese Stateside. Japanese title is *U.F.O. Landed Japan*, with the Japanese issue technically being the first issue, from 1971 (our listing is for *Live*, the most widely known title and attendant cover art). Not issued in the UK. Manufactured by licence from Beacon but not issued in the UK by Beacon. A significant early days two-LP compilation album called *Space Metal* was issued by Nova in 1976. The 12-track package offers selections from all three Mick Bolton-era albums. It is the only UFO compilation of the '70s, with the next significant anthology being *Headstone* from 1983.

Phenomenon

(Chrysalis CHR 1059, May '74)

Side 1: 1. Too Young to Know (Way, Mogg) 3:07; 2. Crystal Light (Schenker, Mogg) 3:44; 3. Doctor Doctor (Schenker, Mogg) 4:10; 4. Space Child (Schenker, Mogg) 3:58; 5. Rock Bottom (Schenker, Mogg) 6:30
Side 2: 1. Oh My (UFO) 2:26; 2. Time on My Hands (Schenker, Mogg) 4:10; 3. Built for Comfort (Dixon) 3:01; 4. Lipstick Traces (Schenker) 2:17; 5. Queen of the Deep (Schenker, Mogg) 5:43
Notes: Michael Schenker replaces Mick Bolton on guitar. The album is preceded by a single pairing the non-LP "Give Her the Gun" and "Sweet Little Thing." Guest performance: Bernie Marsden.

Force It

(Chrysalis CHR 1074, July '75)

Side 1: 1. Let It Roll (Schenker, Mogg) 3:54; 2. Shoot Shoot (UFO) 3:37; 3. High Flyer (Schenker, Mogg) 4:06; 4. Love Lost Love (Schenker, Mogg) 3:19; 5. Out in the Street (Way, Mogg) 5:14
Side 2: 1. Mother Mary (UFO) 3:47; 2. Too Much of Nothing (Way) 3:59; 3. Dance Your Life Away (Schenker, Mogg) 3:31; 4. This Kid's Including Between the Walls (Schenker, Mogg) 6:15
Notes: Different cover arts exist, lending various levels of clarity to the naked couple. Guest performance: Chick Churchill.

No Heavy Petting

(Chrysalis, CHR 1103, May '76)

Side 1: 1. Natural Thing (Schenker, Mogg, Way) 4:00; 2. I'm a Loser (Schenker, Mogg) 3:54; 3. Can You Roll Her (Peyronel, Mogg, Parker) 2:56; 4. Belladonna (Schenker, Mogg) 4:30; 5. Reasons Love (Schenker, Mogg) 3:19
Side 2: 1. Highway Lady (Peyronel) 3:47; 2. On with the Action (Schenker, Mogg) 5:02; 3. A Fool in Love (Miller/Fraser) 2:47; 4. Martian Landscape (Peyronel, Mogg, Parker) 5:08
Notes: The band adds Danny Peyronel on keyboards.

Lights Out

(Chrysalis, CHR 1127, May '77)

Side 1: 1. Too Hot to Handle (Way, Mogg) 3:37; 2. Just Another Suicide (Mogg) 4:57; 3. Try Me (Schenker, Mogg) 4:52); 4. Lights Out (Schenker, Mogg, Parker, Way) 4:31
Side 2: 1. Gettin' Ready (Schenker, Mogg) 3:43; 2. Alone Again Or (Maclean) 2:59; 3. Electric Phase (Way, Mogg, Schenker) 4:24; 4. Love to Love (Schenker, Mogg) 7:02
Notes: Danny Peyronel is replaced by Paul Raymond, who provides keyboards, guitar and vocals.

Obsession

(Chrysalis, CDL 1182, Jun. '78)

Side 1: 1. Only You Can Rock Me (Way, Schenker, Mogg) 4:10; 2. Pack It Up (and Go) (Way, Schenker, Mogg) 3:15; 3. Arbory Hill (Schenker) 1:10; 4. Ain't No Baby (Way, Mogg) 4:00; 5. Lookin' Out for No. 1 (Way, Mogg) 4:35
Side 2: 1. Hot 'n' Ready (Schenker, Mogg) 3:18; 2. Cherry (Way, Mogg) 3:32; 3. You Don't Fool Me (Way, Parker, Mogg) 3:23; 4. Lookin' Out for No. 1 Reprise (Way) 1:18; 5. One More for the Rodeo (Way, Mogg) 3:45; 6. Born to Lose (Schenker, Way, Mogg) 3:33
Notes: Initial UK issue includes poster.

Strangers in the Night

(Chrysalis, CJT 5, Dec. 78)

Side 1: 1. Natural Thing (Schenker, Mogg, Way) 7:05; 2. Out in the Street (Way, Mogg) 9:34; 3. Only You Can Rock Me (Way, Schenker, Mogg) 3:58; 4. Doctor Doctor (Schenker, Mogg) 4:30
Side 2: 1. Mother Mary (UFO) 3:17; 2. This Kid's (Schenker, Mogg) 4:40; 3. Love to Love (Schenker, Mogg) 7:37
Side 3: 1. Lights Out (Schenker, Mogg, Parker, Way) 4:55; 2. Rock Bottom (Schenker, Mogg) 11:02
Side 4: 1. Too Hot to Handle (Way, Mogg) 4:17; 2. I'm a Loser (Schenker, Mogg) 3:49; 3. Let It Roll (Schenker, Mogg) 4:35; 4. Shoot Shoot (UFO) 3:45
Notes: Two-LP live album with gatefold sleeve; 1979 release in North America. UK record labels call the record: *Strangers in the Night: A Double Live Album.*

B. Post-1979 Summary Discography

Note: As food for thought, and as a quick reference, I thought I'd offer an abbreviated, less-detailed discography of UFO's studio albums produced after the period covered in this book. Of course many compilation, live albums and DVDs also saw issue, but I'm drawing the line at this perfunctory checklist of the songs in their original state, so to speak.

No Place to Run (1980)
The Wild, The Willing and the Innocent (1981)
Mechanix (1982)
Making Contact (1983)
Misdemeanor (1985)
Ain't Misbehavin' (1988)
High Stakes & Dangerous Men (1982)
Walk on Water (1995)
Covenant (2000)
Sharks (2002)
You Are Here (2004)
The Monkey Puzzle (2006)
The Visitor (2009)
Seven Deadly (2012)
A Conspiracy of Stars (2015)

Credits

A. Interviews with the Author

Paul Chapman: August 8, 2000, November 21, 2004, 2007, 2015.
Steve Dawson: 2012.
Alex Lifeson: October 3, 2003.
Leo Lyons: December 6, 2004.
Bernie Marsden: April 17, 2002, 2003, June 13, 2013, March 25, 2014.
Phil Mogg: September 22, 2000, January 22, 2004, January 30, 2004, October 11, 2013.
Ron Nevison: 2009, March 4, 2011.
Andy Parker: September 25, 2006, March 16, 2007, May 5, 2009, February 1, 2012, October 11, 2013, January 15, 2015.
Danny Peyronel: September 29, 2004.
Paul Raymond: 2003, September 27, 2004, February 14, 2013.
Michael Schenker: 1999, December 6, 2001, November 7, 2003, September 23, 2004, March 4, 2012, October 18, 2012, December 20, 2013.
Chris Tsangarides: February 17, 2006, 2010.
Pete Way: September 12, 2000, 2002, early 2004, October 3, 2004.

Note: If the above seems a little lacking in detail, it's because some of it is a little hazy, entailing backstage areas and tour buses, where various band members drifted in and out of the conversation. In addition to the above interviews with Phil Mogg, on July 30, 1999, I interviewed on the phone... a Phil Mogg imposter! Within ten seconds of talking to the mystery man, I knew it wasn't Phil, but fascinated, I conducted the interview anyway. Before the summer was out, I was told by a reader that on a flight, someone was impersonating *me*, regaling this reader and his buddy about the writing of all of these rock books. Make of this what you will.

B. Additional Sources

Beat Instrumental. U.F.O A Group of Mystery and Imagination No. 101. September 1971.
Beat Instrumental. UFO Sighted and Identified by Peter Douglas. No. 142. August 1978.
Circus. '*Lights Out*' Lights Up UFO by Peter Crescenti. Issue No.162. August 18, 1977.
Circus. UFO Over America by David Fricke. 1978.
Classic Rock Revisited. Interview with Michael Schenker by Jeb Wright.
Dmme.net. Interview with Phil Mogg by Dmitry Epstein. August 2002.
Goldmine. UFO: tuning in Their Obsessions by Ronald L Smith. No. 36. May 1979.
Guitar for the Practising Musician. Michael Schenker: Past, Present & Future of Euro-Metal by John Stix. Volume 5, No. 1. January 1988.
Guitar 2001. Interview with Michael Schenker. Issue No.10. Summer 2001.

Melody Maker. UFO sighted over Japan by Mike Guy. October 16, 1971.
Melody Maker. *Phenomenon* album review by J.W. May 25, 1974.
Melody Maker. *Force It* album review by E. M. August 8, 1975.
Melody Maker. *Obsession* album review by J.O. August 10, 1978.
Melody Maker. *Strangers in the Night* album review by Harry Doherty. January 20, 1979.
Metal Forces. Back in the Flight by Garry Sharp-Young. Issue 68. January 1992.
Metal-Rules.com. Interviews with Andy Parker, Michael Schenker and Pete Way by Marko Syrjala..
New Musical Express. UFO: 1972 Should Be The Year They Break the British Market by Roger St. Pierre. January 1, 1972.
New Musical Express. *Lights Out* album review by Bob Edmands. June 11, 1977.
New Musical Express. "Can't you turn your bloody spaceship down, mate?" By Bob Edmands. June 29, 1978.
New Musical Express. *Strangers in the Night* album review by Bob Edmands. February 3, 1979.
Pop. UFO vom Pech verfolgt. August 1975.
Pop. UFO in USA by Michael Schenker. July 1976.
Record Collector. The UFO Has Landed by Tim Jones. No. 259. March 2001.
The Rich Davenport Rock Show. Interviews with Michael Schenker and Pete Way.
Rolling Stone. *Phenomenon* album review by Gordon Fletcher. 1974.
Scene. UFO has done it on their own by Cliff Michalski. Vol. 7, No. 25. June 23-29, 1976.
Scene. Case of the missing U.F.O. by Cliff Michalski. Vol. 8, No. 30. August 4-10, 1977.
Sounds. *Phenomenon* album review by P.M. May 1974.
Sounds. *Force It* album review by Geoff Barton. August 9, 1975.
Sounds. *No Heavy Petting* album review by Geoff Barton. May 29, 1976.
Sounds. UFOs: amazing evidence! by Geoff Barton. May 21, 1977.
Sounds. *Lights Out* album review by Geoff Barton. May 28, 1977.
Trouser Press. UFO Over USA by Michael Ameen. No. 35. January 1979.
Waxpaper. UFO Go Full Frontal (But Hands Off, Please) by Joe Robinson. Volume 1, Number 1. May 10, 1976.
Way Ahead. UFO Sighted at Palace by Mike Daley. No. 10. 1977.

About the Author

At approximately 7900 (with over 7000 appearing in his books), Martin has unofficially written more record reviews than anybody in the history of music writing across all genres. Additionally, Martin has penned approximately 73 books on hard rock, heavy metal, classic rock and record collecting. He was Editor In Chief of the now retired Brave Words & Bloody Knuckles, Canada's foremost metal publication for 14 years, and has also contributed to Revolver, Guitar World, Goldmine, Record Collector, bravewords.com, lollipop.com and hardradio.com, with many record label band bios and liner notes to his credit as well. Additionally, Martin has been a regular contractor to Banger Films, having worked for two years as researcher on the award-wining documentary *Rush: Beyond the Lighted Stage*, on the writing and research team for the 11-episode Metal Evolution and on the ten-episode Rock Icons, both for VH1 Classic. Additionally, Martin is the writer of the original metal genre chart used in *Metal: A Headbanger's Journey* and throughout the Metal Evolution episodes. Martin currently resides in Toronto and can be reached through martinp@inforamp.net or www.martinpopoff.com.

Martin Popoff Bibliography

Lights Out: Surviving the '70s with UFO (2018)
AC/DC: Album by Album (2017)
Led Zeppelin: All the Albums, All the Songs (2017)
Tornado of Souls: Thrash's Titanic Clash (2017)
Caught in a Mosh: The Golden Era of Thrash (2017)
Metal Collector: Gathered Tales from Headbangers (2017)
Rush: Album by Album (2017)
Beer Drinkers and Hell Raisers: The Rise of Motörhead (2017)
Hit the Lights: The Birth of Thrash (2017)
Popoff Archive – 4: Classic Rock (2017)
Popoff Archive – 3: Hair Metal (2017)
Popoff Archive – 2: Progressive Rock (2016)
Popoff Archive – 1: Doom Metal (2016)
Rock the Nation: Montrose, Gamma and Ronnie Redefined (2016)
Punk Tees: The Punk Revolution in 125 T-Shirts (2016)
Metal Heart: Aiming High with Accept (2016)
Ramones at 40 (2016)
Time and a Word: The Yes Story (2016)
Kickstart My Heart: A Mötley Crüe Day-by-Day (2015)
This Means War: The Sunset Years of the NWOBHM (2015)
Wheels of Steel: The Explosive Early Years of the NWOBHM (2015)
Swords and Tequila: Riot's Classic First Decade (2015)
Who Invented Heavy Metal? (2015)
Sail Away: Whitesnake's Fantastic Voyage (2015)
Live Magnetic Air: The Unlikely Saga of the Superlative Max Webster (2014)
Steal Away the Night: An Ozzy Osbourne Day-by-Day (2014)
The Big Book of Hair Metal (2014)
Sweating Bullets: The Deth and Rebirth of Megadeth (2014)
  updated and reissued as So Far, So Good... So Megadeth (2017)
Smokin' Valves: A Headbanger's Guide to 900 NWOBHM Records (2014)
The Art of Metal (co-edit with Malcolm Dome; 2013)
2 Minutes to Midnight: An Iron Maiden Day-By-Day (2013)
Metallica: The Complete Illustrated History (2013); update and reissue (2016)
Rush: The Illustrated History (2013); update and reissue (2016)
Ye Olde Metal: 1979 (2013)
Scorpions: Top of the Bill (2013);
  updated and reissued as Wind of Change: The Scorpions Story (2016)
Epic Ted Nugent (2012);
  updated and reissued as Motor City Madhouse: Going Gonzo with Ted Nugent (2017)
Fade to Black: Hard Rock Cover Art of the Vinyl Age (2012)
It's Getting Dangerous: Thin Lizzy 81-12 (2012)

We Will Be Strong: Thin Lizzy 76-81 (2012)
Fighting My Way Back: Thin Lizzy 69-76 (2011);
    updated and reissued as From Dublin to Jailbreak: Thin Lizzy 1969-76 (2016)
The Deep Purple Royal Family: Chain of Events '80 - '11 (2011)
The Deep Purple Royal Family: Chain of Events Through '79 (2011);
    reissued as The Deep Purple Family Year by Year (to 1979) (2016)
Black Sabbath FAQ (2011)
The Collector's Guide to Heavy Metal: Volume 4: The '00s (2011; co-authored with David Perri)
Goldmine Standard Catalog of American Records 1948 - 1991, 7th Edition (2010)
Goldmine Record Album Price Guide, 6th Edition (2009)
Goldmine 45 RPM Price Guide, 7th Edition (2009)
A Castle Full of Rascals: Deep Purple '83 - '09 (2009)
Worlds Away: Voivod and the Art of Michel Langevin (2009)
Ye Olde Metal: 1978 (2009)
Gettin' Tighter: Deep Purple '68 - '76 (2008)
All Access: The Art of the Backstage Pass (2008)
Ye Olde Metal: 1977 (2008)
Ye Olde Metal: 1976 (2008)
Judas Priest: Heavy Metal Painkillers (2007)
Ye Olde Metal: 1973 to 1975 (2007)
The Collector's Guide to Heavy Metal: Volume 3: The Nineties (2007)
Ye Olde Metal: 1968 to 1972 (2007)
Run For Cover: The Art of Derek Riggs (2006)
Black Sabbath: Doom Let Loose (2006)
Dio: Light Beyond the Black (2006)
The Collector's Guide to Heavy Metal: Volume 2: The Eighties (2005)
Rainbow: English Castle Magic (2005)
UFO: Shoot Out the Lights (2005)
The New Wave of British Heavy Metal Singles (2005)
Blue Öyster Cult: Secrets Revealed! (2004); update and reissue (2009);
    updated and reissued as Agents of Fortune: The Blue Oyster Cult Story (2016)
Contents Under Pressure: 30 Years of Rush at Home & Away (2004)
The Top 500 Heavy Metal Albums of All Time (2004)
The Collector's Guide to Heavy Metal: Volume 1: The Seventies (2003)
The Top 500 Heavy Metal Songs of All Time (2003)
Southern Rock Review (2001)
Heavy Metal: 20th Century Rock and Roll (2000)
The Goldmine Price Guide to Heavy Metal Records (2000)
The Collector's Guide to Heavy Metal (1997)
Riff Kills Man! 25 Years of Recorded Hard Rock & Heavy Metal (1993)

See martinpopoff.com for complete details and ordering information.

Martin Popoff titles available from Wymer Publishing:

From Dublin To Jailbreak
Thin Lizzy 1969-76
Martin Popoff

ISBN: 978-1-908724-39-7
Hardback: 256pp,
1 x 8 b/w plate section
RRP: £19.99

Wind Of Change
The Scorpions Story
Martin Popoff

ISBN: 978-1-908724-40-3
Paperback: 256pp,
1 x 8 b/w plate section
RRP: £14.99

Agents Of Fortune
The Blue Öyster Cult Story
Martin Popoff

ISBN: 978-1-908724-41-0
Paperback: 256pp,
1 x 8 b/w plate section
RRP: £14.99

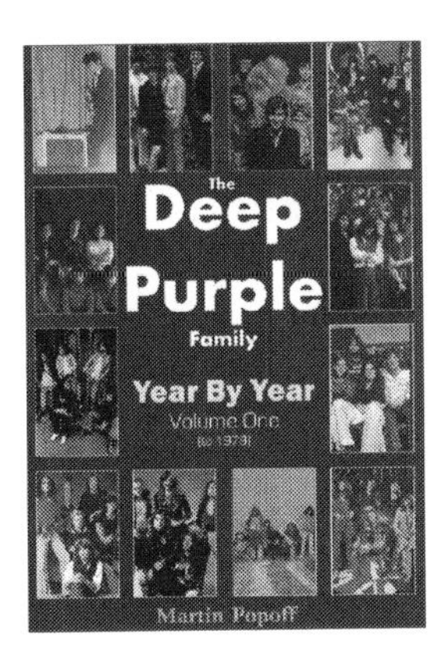

The Deep Purple Family:
Year by Year Vol 1 (- 1979)
Martin Popoff

ISBN: 978-1-908724-42-7
Paperback: 256pp,
Illustrated throughout.
RRP: £14.99

Motor City Madhouse
Going Gonzo with Ted Nugent
Martin Popoff

ISBN: 978-1-908724-59-5
Paperback: 256pp,
1 x 8 b/w plate section
RRP: £14.99

So Far, So Good... So Megadeth!
Martin Popoff

ISBN: 978-1-908724-61-8
Paperback: 288pp
RRP: £14.99

Other titles available from Wymer Publishing:

Frank Talk:
The Inside Stories Of Zappa's Other People
Andrew Greenaway

ISBN: 978-1-908724-67-0
Paperback: 256pp
RRP: £14.99

Chasing Shadows
The Search for Rod Evans
Adrian Jarvis

ISBN: 978-1-908724-65-6
Paperback: 160pp
RRP: £12.99

A Selection Of Shows:
Genesis & Solo Live Guide 1976-2014
Alan Hewitt

ISBN: 978-1-908724-19-9
Paperback: 297 x 210 mm, 224pp
RRP: £24.99

Sketches Of Hackett
The Authorised Steve Hackett Biography
Alan Hewitt

ISBN: 978-1-908724-01-4
Paperback: 356pp
16 photo pages.
RRP: £14.99

T Rextasy - The Spirit Of Marc Bolan
Danielz

ISBN: 978-1-908724-03-8
Paperback: 252pp
(including 64 photo pages)
RRP: £14.99

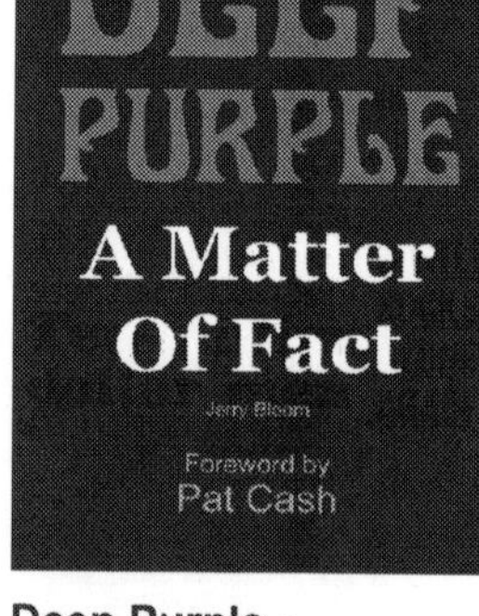

Deep Purple - A Matter of Fact
Jerry Bloom

ISBN: 978-1-908724-06-9
Paperback: 208pp
RRP: £14.99

Anarchy in Britain

ISBN: 978-1-908724-53-3
Paperback: 128pp
RRP: £19.99

The Road of Golden Dust
The Deep Purple Story 1968-76
Jerry Bloom

ISBN: 978-1-908724-23-6
Paperback: 224pp
RRP: £14.99

Zermattitis:
A Musicians' Guide To Going Downhill Fast
Tony Ashton

ISBN: 978-0-9557542-9-6
Hardback: 192pp, Plus DVD
RRP: £24.99

Zappa The Hard Way
Andrew Greenaway

ISBN: 978-1-908724-00-7
Paperback: 210mm x 148 mm, 246 pp, 2 x 16 b/w plates.
RRP: £14.99

A Hart Life
Colin Hart with Dick Allix

ISBN: 978-1-908724-04-5
16 photo pages (87 images)
RRP: £14.99

When Punk Rocked
Andy Francis

ISBN: 978-1-908724-64-9
Paperback: 297 x 210 mm, 128pp
RRP: £19.99